ABOUT THE AUTHOR

After qualifying in 1979, Sheilagh Nisbet enjoyed a number of roles as a vet while raising a family of five and breeding wee Greek horses. In 2015, she gained a master's degree in creative writing, then turned from the absolute truth required in her many papers published in veterinary journals to much more creative writing. She lives near Melrose.

NOT GRAZING BUT BROWSING

SPILLING THE BEANS ON LIFE
AS A WOMAN AND VET

SHEILAGH A NISBET

Matador
9 Priory Business Park,
Wistow Road, Kibworth Beauchamp,
Leicestershire. LE8 0RX
Tel: 0116 279 2299
Email: books@troubador.co.uk
Web: www.troubador.co.uk/matador
Twitter: @matadorbooks

ISBN 978 1800462 717

British Library Cataloguing in Publication Data.
A catalogue record for this book is available from the British Library.

Printed and bound in Great Britain by 4edge Limited
Typeset in 11pt Minion Pro by Troubador Publishing Ltd, Leicester, UK

Matador is an imprint of Troubador Publishing Ltd

In memory of Rosemary Dale

CONTENTS

Acknowledgements

It should be noted that some of the practices and procedures I have described at my various former workplaces have been superseded.

The events I have recounted are written as I remember them but memory can play tricks and although how I felt about these situations is factual, some of the details no doubt have been blurred by time and distance.

To preserve the privacy of those who may not wish to be identified, I have used pseudonyms and changed other personal details in many of my stories. However, I would like to leave the reader in no doubt that were it not for the men and women featured in this book, as well as many others I don't mention, people whose leg I may gently pull yet whom I remember with fondness, gratitude and enormous admiration, my journey thus far through life would have been impoverished and homogeneous. That said, I am sorry if anyone feels misrepresented.

During my research for this book, to assist, where necessary, accuracy of details and for background information, I referred to the resources listed in the Bibliography.

Writing is a long and lonesome journey. I am indebted to my tutors and fellow students of the Open University's Master's degree in Creative Writing, people who inspired and encouraged my writing efforts and, in turn, from whose writing I learned so much. I am also grateful to Denis Ostler, a former senior colleague in the Veterinary Investigation Service, for his encouragement to write and for the advice he gave me many years ago that whatever you decide to do with your life, it is imperative that you find it fun. Linda Smith and John Harte kindly reviewed the manuscript, and my loyal writing companion has been Oscar, my whippet, without whom I would have found writing infinitely more arduous.

1

Whippets and wider relevance: A Prologue

So, to bring my memoirs to life, for sure a fictional masterpiece to rival *Gone with the wind*, Rebus and anything JK turns out, I need up to date and scenic detail of a modern, state-of the-art veterinary practice: what are the vaccine protocols these days, the 'go-to' antibiotics, how are recurrent itchy skins managed, what about bad debts, and how do you get to retirement with all your marbles and a degree of optimism.

I pull up in the car park, being careful to avoid the odd pothole, next to a sign depicting a dog, a dog turd and a big, red cross through the latter. Paddy is standing at the practice door, roll up in his left hand, scrolling through his phone with the other. He looks up and waves as I approach. The brass plaque beside the entrance bearing the words, in black letters, 'Patrick Gillon BVMS MRCVS Veterinary

Surgeon', needs a good clean and is tatty around the edges, a wee bit like poor Paddy himself.

'Sheilagh', he yells across the yard, dropping the fag end on the ground, rubbing his foot on it, then, with apparent second thoughts, picking it up and putting it in the bin for bagged dog poo. 'Been a long time. Too long.'

I nod as I approach then we give each other one of those no hug hugs where the only parts of your body that make contact with the other's are the under surface of the arms and the shoulders. He smells of tobacco and I see dandruff on his frayed shirt collar.

Paddy and I graduated from Glasgow the same year and over the forty odd years since then we've had occasional contact, charting each other's journeys through work, marriage, children, divorce, more work, re-marriage, more children – you get the picture. It's just gone noon, so he suggests we go to the Horse and Hound for an early lunch.

'So how're things in practice?' I ask after ordering a lime and soda for Paddy, still mineral water for myself and the menu.

Paddy shrugs. 'All right. It'll see me through. Been a few changes, of course, since you left to join "the dark side",' he gives me a slow wink, 'and we're blooming grateful for pet insurance. What about you?'

'Oh, I think I made a reasonable go at government work,' I answer, taking the menu from the barman and pulling the glass of mineral water towards me. 'Took some adapting to state veterinary medicine, but it was interesting and allowed time for home life as well.'

'Yeah, not much of that in practice,' Paddy shakes his head and takes a gulp of limed soda.

I glance at the menu. 'What's an eight-inch hoagie?' I ask Paddy.

He looks at me and shrugs. 'No idea. Wish I had one, though.'

'Ah, the Gillon humour hasn't waned.' I smile and touch his shoulder.

'Not sure I'd have survived without it, Sheilagh.' He smiles back then glances into the green depths of his glass. 'Do you still keep in touch with anyone else in our year? What happened to that wanker Elliot?'

'Ivan? Running a smart outfit in Kensington, last I heard.'

'Making big bananas, then,' Paddy says, his tone resembling the colour of his drink.

'He'll be doing okay. Did you hear about Ruth what's-her-name?'

'Morgan? The one with the big teeth we called "horse"?'

I nod. 'Yes, that's her. Married an American horse whisperer and living in Arizona luxury.'

We order two hoagies then eat them as we continue to gossip over mutual acquaintances, interspersed with rose-tinged reminiscences of Glaswegian seventies life, all flares and platforms and Lanliq.

'Afternoon surgery's about to start,' Paddy says as we walk back to his practice, 'so I can't show you round, but you're welcome to have a quick look if you like.'

I have a quick look. The smell is the same as practices I worked in always had – a curious blend of pine disinfectant, medicine cabinets and Bovril. The vinyl floors haven't changed, nor the multi-tasking nurses. A dog gives a desultory bark from behind a door and there's a woman at the desk arguing with the receptionist over her bill. The epitome of middle class yet impecunious elegance, the woman places her cat basket on the floor, freeing her hands for a more emphasised complaint. I shudder. How I do not miss that.

Suddenly, I feel tired. This immersive research has been more like a witch's dunking. I decide I've enough detail to be going on with, wave through the consulting window to Paddy and head for my car.

'Veterinary trials and tribulations, cairn terriers and why we should trim hedges: veterinary memoir or not?'

I'd given Paddy a draft of my book. He'd said he would read it over a wet weekend while #wifethree and #familytwo were away at Centreparcs for the school holidays, and he was 'more than willing' to tell me what he thought. As ever, I knew I could rely on his ingenuousness. He went on, in comic critic's comportment.

'If you read only one veterinary memoir this year, make it this one. Destined to sit amongst the shelves of best-sellers. Don't wait for the paperback, this is a must-read.'

I laughed at his leg-pulling, simultaneously pleased that he appeared to have read my first literary attempt.

'It is memoir, I take it? Or what are you calling this epistle, Sheilagh? Autobiography, or something a bit more punchy, didactic?'

'Obviously not an epistle, Paddy. That means letters, doesn't it. And has biblical overtures …'

'… the gospel according to Chicken,' Paddy interjected, using the undoubtedly affectionate nickname bestowed on me by my colleagues at Glasgow Vet School on account of the size of my nose relative to the rest of my face. That and the skinny legs.

'… and which I would aim to avoid,' I said, managing a smile. 'Autobiography is more straightforward fact than an interpretation of facts as I remember them – that's more the province of memoir, but I've included quite a lot of musing over certain conundrums. Conundra?'

Paddy shrugged and took a mouthful of the coffee I'd prepared for him. He swallowed, screwed up his eyes and opened his mouth wide.

'What have you put in it?' he yelped.

'A bit of milk, no sugar, like you asked.'

Paddy shook his head as if trying to free his ears of water after a swim.

I tasted my coffee. Nothing untoward. 'What's the matter?' I asked, frowning.

'Is it UHT? It's effing UHT, isn't it?'

I nodded.

We were outside my garden shed where I'd thrashed out my reminiscences, and had settled down in the Lloyd loom chairs I'd seen on Gumtree and then painted in a lurid vomit-yellow. Oscar, my whippet and writing companion and 'hardly a real dog' according to the UHT-hater, had snuggled down on the duvet I'd provided for him on the grass beside us.

'Sorry to disappoint, Paddy. The cat had the last of the fresh stuff. Anyway, you were telling me what you thought about my draft.'

With a thump that woke Oscar, Paddy put his mug on the grass, stretched out his legs then crossed them at the ankles and looked at me, still scowling. 'Question is, does the world need another veterinary memoir?'

Ouch. Straight for the jugular. I look back, wide-eyed. 'Well ...'

'I mean,' Paddy continued his brutal review, 'ever since Alf Wight put pen to paper and published his fantastically successful Herriot stories,' Paddy spread his arms and opened his palms, 'everyone with an MRCVS seems to want to follow suit, certain that their efforts will be as well-received as Wight's. None of them has. Not. One,' Paddy ended his diatribe pointing his finger to the beat of his prose.

Pity I hadn't gone to the Co-op for milk that morning.

'I don't think the billions of people who share this planet with me will suffer if there isn't another book about a vet. That's true,' I said, smiling and nodding.

I sat down on the grass with Oscar and played with his ears.

'Why don't you like whippets?' I asked.

Paddy shrugged and grimaced. 'They've no presence. Don't seem to have any self-respect. If you had a springer or a Labrador or even a collie, you'd know what I mean.'

'I think I know what you mean. But that's why I like whippets. They ask for nothing.'

Bramble, my cat, the lack of whom may have meant a

more amenable reviewer, strolled across the drive. Oscar leaped from his duvet and onto the tabby, grabbed him by the head with his jaws then tried to twist it off.

I smiled and shook my head. 'Ozzy,' I called, like a mother to a toddler who's refusing to share his toys, 'be nice to the kitty.'

'"Be nice to the kitty",' Paddy mimicked in high, mocking tones. 'Look what he's doing, for heaven's sake.'

Paddy was clearly alarmed by the sight of a whippet dragging a cat over gravel by the neck.

'Bramble can take care of himself. Watch,' I replied.

The cat seized his chance when Oscar stopped for breath, reared up on his hind legs and boxed the dog's face, claws bared. Oscar yelped and ran back to join us. I patted him on the head, got up from the grass and sat down in my Lloyd loom and continued.

'I suppose what might give my writing an appeal beyond amusing veterinary stories is a wider relevance I've tried to give it.'

I helped Oscar on to my lap, settled him down then looked at Paddy. He looked back, lowering his head.

'Wider relevance? Sounds like you've taken this creative writing gobbledygook seriously.'

I smiled and chuckled. With friends like Paddy, arrogance and egoism were beyond my grasp.

'Well, yes, I have. But I don't know what I'd do without your reality checks, Paddy.'

'So, you think there's something in your book that people, other than your family and long-suffering friends, will want to read?'

'Uh-huh. Well, maybe,' I said, sensing a thaw in my friend's approach. 'I mean, that was what I aimed for, you know, a sort of story about how I've got through life so far not just as a vet, because actually most of the time I was bringing up the kids, you know, being a parent. Lots of people are doing that and they might empathise, you know, feel they can relate to my experiences.'

Paddy had turned to look at the drive bordering the grass needing cutting and the daisies casting long shadows in the early evening summer sunlight. His head was moving slowly up and down in a contemplative way and I allowed myself to consider that he was reviewing a few of the life experiences we'd had in common and he'd begun to see how my book had helped him make sense of them.

'You've a problem with moles, Sheilagh.'

Such bathos. I squirmed, then smiled and chuckled at my self-importance. Paddy turned to look at me.

'No, look, over there,' he pointed to the turf near the gate, 'two molehills already and they won't stop there, I can tell you.'

I took a deep breath to stem my embarrassed mirth. 'You're right. I'll get it sorted.'

'How are your kids, anyway?' Paddy asked turning to look at the jilted lawn again.

I knew he wouldn't want a blow by blow account of what each of the kids was doing along the lines of these 'dear blank' typed letters that you occasionally find lurking in Christmas cards.

'They're fine, thanks. All grown up, of course. With a few grown up problems, too,' I smiled at Paddy.

'Yup, but that's part of the deal. Same with my older kids,' he said, still looking at the grass.

I nodded, took Oscar's left front paw and inspected the toes and claws.

'Knocked-up toe. That's another problem with these ridiculous breeds,' Paddy said, frowning at my hound.

'Which one?' I asked. 'His toes are okay, aren't they?'

Paddy nodded. 'I was just saying.'

I smiled. 'Tell you what, let's go into town and I'll treat you to a Chinese and some proper coffee before you head home.'

'Make it Indian and I'll give you a few tips for your extensive re-drafting.

2

NOT WITHOUT MISS McCROSTY

'His name's Buddy,' Uncle Alec said to me over his ample belly and from an armchair with fringing around the armrests like a cowboy's shirt. 'Do you like him, Sheilagh?'

I nodded and stroked the head of the dog sitting beside me.

It was around the time I started joined-up writing, and my parents had dragged my sister Val, brother Robin and me to Edinburgh to see relatives. This would consume the whole of Saturday, our only day off in each week with the churn of the school timetable and Sunday the possession of church and homework.

The relatives lived in a damp, mothball-infused house in Ferry Road. Auntie Jean, a beanpole of a medical secretary, answered the door and tailgated us in, and, as she bent down to kiss me, I could tell she'd absorbed the house's odours. Rubbing her saliva off my face, I saw her rough-haired fox terrier. Back then I felt shy with people and had more kinship with animals, warming to their wordless communication of friendship and absence of expectations to say something when I could think of nothing beyond the monosyllabic.

So I'd joined Buddy on the mat in front of the two-bar electric fire with red light bulbs and rotating metal whirligigs that gave the impression of real flames; a sort of mid-twentieth century *hygge*. When there was a lull in the grown-ups' conversation Auntie Jean looked down towards me, back to my mother and broke the silence with 'looks like she'll be a vet then, Isobel,' and Mum agreed that maybe I would.

'What's a vet?' I asked from the back of the car on the way home, watching the reflection of the lights from the Forth Road Bridge turn the river beneath into sequinned satin.

'A doctor for animals,' Dad replied, and I thought yes, that's what I'll be.

The first woman vet was Aleen Cust. Although she studied veterinary medicine and qualified in 1900, the Royal College of Veterinary Surgeons refused to admit her as a member. However, she returned to her native Ireland to work as a vet's assistant. With the outbreak of World War 1, she travelled to France and volunteered to treat the Army's horses, and it was only in 1922, after the Sex Disqualification (Removal) Act, that the RCVS admitted Cust as a member.

Cust's biographer, Connie Ford, whom I had the honour of meeting and who was another courageous woman who fought for the right to be educated and join the veterinary profession was, along with Cust, inspirational to women aspiring to be vets.

The situation improved, with the number of women being admitted to veterinary schools gradually increasing, however by the 1970s when I was applying for university, it hadn't occurred to me that my gender would be disadvantageous. But, as Darwin noted, ignorance begets confidence.

Hans and Lotte were my first pets and I couldn't tell which was which. For reasons I never knew, except that he was keen on anything teutonic, my Dad named them after Austrian scuba divers. They held my interest for a few seconds at a time, swimming in their goldfish bowl with that opening and closing of the mouth that people do in dentist chairs and I found it difficult to form a relationship with them. But it was rewarding to throw in the meaty-smelling fish food, see them swoop up and envelope the crumbs with their wide-open gummy mouths.

'Cup your hands together and hold them till I fill the bowl,' Dad said to me when he changed the water.

I watched the fish in their sliminess wriggling in my hands, doing their mouth thing and squirming like the fortune-telling bits of cellophane inside Christmas crackers. The smell of dank ponds with fishy top notes took ages to wash from my skin. As in the best long partnerships, they died within hours of each other and Mum flushed them down the loo.

'Can I please have a rabbit now?' I asked, watching Hans and Lotte whirlpool round in the bowl then disappear.

'No, silly,' Mum replied, 'have you forgotten Timmy's coming to live with us? You won't have time for a rabbit.'

Uncle Jim had been posted to Singapore with the Royal Air Force and Mum stepped in, offering his Boxer dog a home.

'Have you given him beer again?' Mum scolded her little brother as she wiped froth from Timmy's mouth.

Jim shrugged. He had brought his dog to us via the local pub, a place that my Baptist upbringing regarded with abomination.

'Pat him nicely,' Mum said to Val, Robin and me when Jim had gone.

Timmy's coat was velvet in my hands. His sweet chestnuts of eyes met mine and I knew we'd be friends. He drooled from the corners of his mouth; stringy coils of saliva that wouldn't wash out of my hair and left slug trails over my shoes, but we were both four years old and would grow up together, singing from the same hymn sheet and I loved him. Less so did our neighbours whom Timmy, cold turkey with beer withdrawal, visited, waiting outside each house door until someone came out with a biscuit.

'Get your uniform and satchel ready for tomorrow,' was Mum's Sunday evening mantra to ensure efficient use of time before the hour-long morning bus journey to school.

The prospect of another school week with ten hours of bus travel coiled like a boa-constrictor round my intestines, but I'd curl up with Timmy in his basket and he'd lick my face and understand what my parents could not.

As we approached our tenth summer, Timmy became ill and Dad said no vet can cure old age. Timmy died one evening after I had gone to bed and I found him in the morning where Dad had laid him, wrapped in a blanket outside. I kissed his cold head, sobbed as if all my school Mondays had come at once and for a while afterwards was suffused with a melancholy not wholly lifted when Mum said, 'You can have a rabbit now.'

We got two rabbits. Robin's one, Mac, was a light brown doe and I called mine Sooty, a black doe with white fur around her eyes. When Mac had babies we realised that mine must be a buck but that didn't matter as Sooty can be a boy's name, too.

'What are you looking for?' Mum asked Dad as he climbed up the shaky aluminium ladders and disappeared into our loft.

'More rabbit-room,' Dad said as he descended with a tea chest.

Mum shook her head.

Dad water-proofed the outside with creosote, the smell of which for many years gave me a simultaneous feel of rabbit fur, and made a door out of chicken wire. We put in wood shavings for bedding and soon Mac and Sooty were great-grandparents.

When there wasn't a household in the village that didn't own some of our rabbits, by comparing Mac and Sooty's furry nether regions, I learned how to tell a boy rabbit from a girl rabbit. As Pasteur remarked, 'In the field of observation, chance favours the mind that is prepared,' and I thus brought the breeding programme under control.

Motivated with this success, I looked up 'vet' in the threadbare copy of Chambers that always lay on top of the bookcase in the hall of our house and saw that it was short for veterinary surgeon. Adding to the allure of working with species which shared my wavelength was the sound of the title with its lyrical rhythm, multiple syllables and so many 'R's. It was as covetable as the company of animals themselves.

During a school lunch when I was a few years older, the teacher at my table, Miss Fotheringham, asked us what we'd like to be when we grew up. She was groomed to precision with jaw length, dark hair and wore her blouses buttoned up to her neck. Walking outside the school, she'd hunch her shoulders, corrugate her brow and wrap her teacher's gown around her chest, folding her arms and pointing the toes of her sensible flats outwards with every purposeful step. I doubt she wanted to know our career plans, and suspect it was more a lesson in making solicitous conversation at meal times, in between dainty mouthfuls of hot pot while you rest your cutlery on the plate then place your hands on your lap.

We ate school meals in an old drill hall. It had long windows that stretched up to the ceiling and the single-glazing gave the thermal protection of flip-flops in snow. Regardless of the menu, the hall smelled of dried vegetable soup, although that wasn't the variety served. I abhorred soup day. This meant that cold boiled brisket, the juices of which were probably used to make the soup, was served and accompanied by gravestones of bread, the harbinger of my hated meal. Some of us would roll and squash the dough into cricket ball density and throw it to others before the teachers arrived.

'I'll be an eventer,' said Tingy, wriggling on the bottom-bruising bench where we girls sat, three each side of the wooden table with a teacher at the head.

My best pal for many years, Tingy hoped for fame in this equestrian sport and her mother also encouraged her to keep goats which Tingy milked twice daily, endowing her with musky and muscular hands. Each morning, she strangled her rat-tail hair into plaits, and refused to wear make-up at school dances, the one event in the school calendar when this was permitted. Tingy and I shared a wiriness and simian tendencies around trees but we drifted apart when she prepared for Burghley and I for boys.

Rhoda, also horsey, nodded towards Tingy and said over the chatter and clatter of nearby tables, 'I'd like to be a show jumper.'

Blonde Barbara, the first of us to wear a bra, raised her eyebrows. 'I think I'd be good at beauty therapy,' she opined, her eyes oozing lustfulness as she glanced across the wooden floor towards the boys' tables on the other side of the hall and fiddled with the thick pony tail that reached her coccyx.

Only at the Form Six tables were the genders permitted to sit together and without a member of teaching staff. I suppose it was preparation for the stage in our education beyond school and to immunise us against the otherwise inevitable moral ruin when opposite sexes mix unchaperoned.

Bouncy Barbara with the short ginger curls and freckles that coalesced like bacterial colonies wanted to be a doctor. I can't remember precisely what Fiona said. She loved cats so perhaps she found a means of indulging her feline fancies.

'What about you, Sheilagh?' Miss Fotheringham asked with a patient smile and sideways tilt of her head. 'What will you be?'

Always last to contribute to conversations, I swallowed a chunk of lamb fat, inhaled the soupy smell and looked up. 'A vet-er-in-ar-y sur-geon,' I replied, savouring each syllable.

'Vet'rinary surgeon, we say,' said Miss Fotheringham, nodding her head and briefly closing her eyes.

Although it meant dropping one of these nice syllables, I liked the neatness of the proper pronunciation and I practised it under my breath all the way home on the St Andrews bus, as it belched climate-changing gases with every gear change.

When she later married Mr Morris, a maths teacher, Miss Fotheringham resigned, as did many of her contemporaries on tying the knot, and became a mother of three. I, however, never wavered from my veterinary ambition. Except, that is, for a brief yet bewildering interlude when I changed schools, discovered Embassy Regal and began to understand the sort of interest in boys first shown to me by Blonde Barbara. As the mist around teenage attractions cleared, the path to veterinary medicine seemed blurred and blooming hard work.

It was at the following senior school Christmas dance that we poured a quarter bottle of Bacardi into an empty bottle, some friends and I, and topped it up with lemonade; the epitome of clandestine insurrection and the power to make Jimmy Shand's country dance band sound as cool as Roxy Music. This prototype Alcopops tasted like a cross between cream soda and Christmas pudding sauce, and took all of five minutes to drink. Through a rummy mist and spirited enactment of The Dashing White Sergeant with Adrian, a near-exotic boy in fifth year – he was born in Burma although his parents moved to Brentwood – I thought, sod it, it takes a lot of work to get the four As at Higher grade for vet school entrance; I'll emulate Darwin instead.

Next morning, as I struggled with a sledgehammer cracking down on my head to my heart's rhythm, Darwin's appeal was even stronger, and the allure of taking myself off on a Beagle-like voyage to some little-known island to discover a new species of tree-dwelling amphibian helped sooth the symptoms of the previous night's excesses. But also appealing was the after-school socialising, made possible by my family's move from the country into the town. Sharing a knickerbocker glory with Val and some pals in Carly's cafe followed by a daundering walk home, hand-in-hand with Adrian, instead of dashing back to saturate myself in assiduous after-school learning, seemed more humane.

But it all came to an end one drizzly afternoon when an elderly member of the town's presbytery brought a complaint to the headmistress. I was hauled in to face the music the following day.

'Sheilagh, you caused Miss McCrosty great offence yesterday,' the headmistress said, flaring her nostrils, widening her eyes and raising her brow.

I had no idea what I'd done to the old lady. I frowned at them both.

'Yes, indeed, Agnes,' Miss McCrosty confirmed to the headmistress, whom I later learned was her old school pal. 'This was a disgraceful incident,' she added, shaking her head so hard the pheasant feathers in her hat trembled.

I tried hard to think what on Earth I'd been doing to deserve this account, but Miss McCrosty did not hesitate to provide the lurid detail.

'I had to step off the pavement to pass them,' she said, exaggerating her annunciation of the triple 'P' to emphasise her disgust.

I was waiting for the punchline when the headmistress stepped in and insisted I apologise for the heinous crime of being too engrossed in talking to Adrian to notice that Miss McCrosty couldn't get passed us. Astonishingly, this wasn't the end of the matter; it was followed up with an interview with my pastoral teacher.

'We expect better of girls like you, Sheilagh,' Miss Harvester said with a look that suggested she'd detected an offensive odour. 'You used to work so hard for your exams. What is it you want to do when you leave school?'

Seething through this chorus of opprobrium, I considered the response to the whole episode was akin to having your hand chopped off for pinching a Mars bar from RS McColl. Although stealing is indeed a crime; unintentionally causing an elderly member of the community of indisputable moral rectitude to step off the pavement, however impolite, was not illegal. I shrugged my shoulders and shuffled my feet. Biology, probably, I murmured to the floor. Maybe veterinary medicine. Dunno.

'You are quite capable of veterinary medicine,' Miss Harvester said with a sniff.

This made me look up. Despite the delivery that would have made Jean Brodie beam, Miss Forester had expressed a belief in my ability to be a vet that hitherto had been the sole province of Aunty Jean and my parents. Everyone else had responded to my aspirations with raised eyebrows, lips pursed till they resembled a cat's anus, head shakes and a clear steer towards human medicine. Remember, this was the early 1970s when veterinary medicine was one of the last male enclaves and generally considered as appropriate and desirable a career for women as pole dancing, stripping or working in a brothel. 'You're quite capable of veterinary medicine,' I repeated to myself as I left Miss Forester's office and closed the door softly.

I walked home without Adrian and with a leap into the gutter whenever I met someone with more than a few wrinkles and grey hairs. Studying zoology and genetics and looking for tree frogs would also be tough and I would probably get seasick on the way; and Darwin had had a rough time with a tumultuous personal life; and he was vilified by eminent peers; and he was immortalised in irreverent cartoons. It all made sense. All hail, Miss Harvester. Bless you, Miss McCrosty.

I started fifth year the following September with renewed veterinary ambitions. Adrian had returned to

Brentwood to build on the unshakeable foundations of his Scottish education, making time, ice-cream and Embassy Regal in Carly's less rewarding. I reverted to plan A, got my head down, studied hard and never touched Bacardi again.

3

LES ÉCOSSAISES

Liz, my flat mate, is frowning as she rips the top off a pot of yoghurt.

'Are you saying that on the word of a drunken bum, you're proposing to drag me across the Channel to some French place in the sticks? A drunk-en bum,' she repeats each syllable while stabbing her spoon into the treat she has promised herself since breakfasting on black coffee eight hours ago.

'Malcolm isn't a drunken bum,' I say wiping a splash of yoghurt from the table top. 'We were enjoying a few beers when he told me about his granny's friend who went to Uni with a French lady who owns a farm near Amiens. Malcolm did his farm experience there and had a great time and when I said you and I ...'

'Hang on,' Liz interrupts, scraping out the last molecules of yoghurt with her forefinger and frowning, 'the contact is this drunk's granny's friend's friend? Bit convoluted and how can she be a farmer – must be at least seventy.'

An age that is a heartbeat from the crematorium.

Trish and Eileen, our two flatmates, arrive. They're both doing medicine – easier than our veterinary studies because they only learn about one species and it talks. Mostly. I tell them about my proposal to do a French placement.

'Wonderful. I love Paris. The cafés, waiters, the whole … ambience,' fantasises Trish.

'Uh huh,' I shrug, 'but we'd be in the country …'

'The sticks,' interjects Liz.

'… and we wouldn't see many waiters. But we'd get valuable livestock experience.'

Trish raises her eyebrows and bends her head to one side. 'Sounds like a good idea then.'

Liz gazes into her empty yoghurt pot.

Eileen points out that learning foreign languages is known to improve brain capacity and sharpen mental acuity; good things as we get nearer to final exams. Trish agrees and reminds us that we haven't been successful in arranging this part of extramural studies yet, and the French proposal is better than nothing.

I'm grateful for the support from Trish and Eileen but go to the fridge for a pot of yoghurt and offer it to Liz. It works. She is persuaded.

'Oh, all right then. But if it's as bad as I fear, and I ever meet this drunken bum …'

'It won't be. And I'll make sure you don't,' I promise.

I remember we're out of coffee.

'I'm popping to the Spar. Can I get you some more yoghurt, Liz?'

'Anything with zero calories,' she mooches.

The train from Calais has pulled into Amiens and I muster every atom of my French O level to ring the farm. Adrianne, the drunk's granny's friend's friend's daughter-in-law drives Liz and me in her old Citroën to the farm, covering the thirty kilometres of winding roads in half the minutes.

We introduce ourselves. Adrianne speaks like she drives.

'*Il vous faut parler en Francais*,' she dictates, forbidding English, except when we're with her children whom we must teach our language. She is slim, muscular and thirty-five years old; mother to Delphine, Mathieu, Pascal and Aysseline, aged two to twelve years; history teacher at a local *lycée*, tennis champion and wife of Hugo who runs the farm.

She asks what we want to learn from our visit and when we tell her about the livestock experience we need, she frowns, shakes her head and exclaims, 'Don't you want to learn about our culture, our language? To get to know us and our friends?' She hits the steering wheel and finishes her diatribe just short of a French expletive.

Liz is in the back of the car clutching the vinyl seat every time Adrianne swerves. She looks pale. I smile. She scowls back.

Hugo is small and wiry. He moves, eats and speaks with the leisure of landed gentry.

'*Le cochon, Lees. Veuillez obtenir de lui*,' he asks Liz, with a small bow of the head and I think of the comparable instruction I got on an Aberdeenshire farm, 'Grab that pig, hen.'

Hugo often smiles and refers to us as *les écossaises,* the Scottish girls, even though Liz is from Saltburn-by-sea. We fit into his five hour working day on the farm, broken up by a four-hour lunch break, when we must converse with the family and their friends.

'*Bonjour*,' Hugo greets us each morning after our breakfast of warm milk and baguette. Then, '*eh bien*,' before he describes our work for the day, more like a tour guide to tourists than a farmer to students.

In the evenings, Adrianne has more friends round.

'*Shaylaah, Lees, c'est Emmanuelle*,' she introduces us to everyone. She checks regularly to make sure we're speaking with someone. Liz says finishing school must be easier.

Not only the farm but the adjacent château have been in Hugo's family for generations and his parents and sister Madalene and her family live in the wing at right angles to Hugo and Adrianne's wing.

'*Le café de Madalene*,' we hear Adrianne complain about her caffeine-induced insomnia one night at three am. I wonder if these in-laws are at odds.

The roads around the château have yellow gravel. Ivy covers the white stone walls and there are rainbows of wallflowers with an inescapable perfume. The rooms smell of damp. The walls have sepia pictures of people in Victorian clothes and one of a soldier on horseback.

The television is the size of a cornflakes packet and kept in a cupboard. This doesn't bother us because in our spare time Liz and I read our book on pig husbandry.

'I'm going to ask Hugo if they do any AI,' I say, 'What's artificial insemination in French?'

'Le boar in la bottle,' muses Liz.

Our planks of beds have bolsters instead of pillows but after a day of building relationships, insomnia does not trouble us.

Liz and I are sitting on a wooden bench by the tennis court where Delphine is playing in a children's tournament. I admire that all her family are here, taking *les écossaises*.

Hugo's father sits down on the bench to the other side of me, nodding a greeting to us. He exhales and mixed with his body odour, I smell *Gauloise* and alcohol. I glance at his amber profile.

Delphine serves an ace. We all clap. During a ping pong of relay, I feel a hand go up my back. It's Liz having a joke. I turn to her, freezing as I see both her hands in her lap. I swing round and stare at the old man. He withdraws his hand looking at me as if I were something a dog did on the carpet. Delphine brings the awkwardness to a close by breaking her opponent's serve.

We're tired when we get back to the château, so limit reading the pig book to a page on weaning.

I tell Liz about the grandfather. 'I'm probably being too sensitive.'

Liz shrugs. 'He's a dirty old man, but there's probably no French for that.'

'Did Delphine win?' I ask, realising that I hadn't concentrated much.

'Yes, her team won,' smiled Liz.

I resolve to be more robust and to congratulate Delphine in the morning.

It's Adrianne's dinner party and Liz and I are sitting in jeans and T shirts. Besides Hugo and his parents there's an Apollo and Aphrodite of a couple. She's the daughter of a French politician, I glean. Apollo's eyes of cloudless sky meet mine. He smiles. My beats per minute reach zillions.

'So. Shaylaah,' Heck, he's saying my name, 'you aaarr a stoodawn?'

'*En Francais, s'il vous plaît,*' Adrianne chides.

I oblige. '*Oui, une étudiante vétérinaire. Liz, aussi.*'

'*Aaaah. Lees aussi,*' he moves the sky to Liz and recreates the palpitating look.

Aphrodite gives a stillborn smile and crosses her legs that go up to her diaphragm. She adjusts an unimpeachable lock over her eye and chats to Hugo, liquidising him.

Mathieu and Pascal appear. They smile at Liz and me, kindred spirits in this forum, and we're pleased to speak English. Adrianne moves to evict them but Aphrodite gives a welcoming wave of Versace. Mathieu is wearing his magician's cloak over his pyjamas and carries a black wand.

'Will you show us a trick, Mathieu?' I ask.

'*Attendez,*' he replies and when I give a mock frown, he corrects himself, 'Wait, please.'

Pascal takes a pack of cards from his dressing gown pocket and asks Liz to pick one. Mathieu and Pascal consider the cards, nod to each other, then Mathieu correctly announces the card that Liz chose. We all clap.

Adrianne shakes her head. '*Un clown.*'

'*Un clown intelligent, Adrianne,*' I suggest.

She nods and, for the first time, gives me a smile and says thank you. I glow.

'Goodnight, Mathieu. Goodnight, Pascal,' Liz and I say as the boys return to their bedroom.

They smile and say goodnight and *bonne nuit.*

We have five courses: a clear beef soup, green beans from the grandfather's garden (*al dente* and with a herb dressing) and then, using our same plate wiped clean with baguette, we have rabbit casserole, including its head which Hugo's mother tucks into. After this there is Emmental, Brie and a soft goat's cheese and then a pot of set custard.

I begin to like the emphasis on nurturing friendships and how Hugo and Adrianne sit not at the ends of the table but in the middle amongst their guests, and how everyone speaks and listens simultaneously, and that it is polite to put your elbows on the table; and how we conclude with tiny cups of coffee and a bottle of single malt that Hugo keeps locked away in a wooden chest.

We haven't found time to read the pig book, but I curl up in bed that night, after replacing the bolster with a cushion, and thanking Liz for agreeing to come with me here. I also decide that if I flunk the vet course I'll marry a French farmer and raise a clutch of kids amongst rare breed pigs.

4

FILLET WITH BOLLINGER

'Miss Nisbet,' Donald called to me from across the yard after a morning at Linton Stud, 'it has come to my attention that female veterinary students never pee. Is this true?'

My face felt warmer than the blood samples I had just taken from a mare. I didn't know what to say. I shook my head.

'Oh, you do pee?' Donald was enjoying the grins of the grooms. 'Then you may use the office facility while I nip behind this shed.'

Inverness-born Donald Fraser, one of Lincolnshire's equine vets, had agreed to my spending four weeks' extramural studies with him. My purpose was to gain first hand experience of veterinary practice and I welcomed the unintended experiences as I would a 'Glasgow kiss'.

I said little during the drive back to Lincoln. On our return to the surgery we found Peter, the other senior vet, and Gill, their assistant, in the general office.

'Sophie is asking for four weeks' holiday in November to visit her relatives in Australia,' Peter said to Donald after the usual hellos and comments on the weather.

'And who does the lovely Sophie propose will cover her nursing duties while she cavorts around the Antipodes?' Donald challenged, with an ominous annunciation of each syllable.

Donald referred to all the veterinary nurses with the pre-nominals, 'the lovely'. I was surprised to hear no one object; even back in 1977, his condescension was anachronistic. Peter and Gill exchanged glances and Donald went down the corridor to his office. Peter followed him.

'Oh dear,' Gill said, watching Peter leave, 'maybe another brawl on the way.' She looked at me and smiled. 'After one of their to-do's, Peter left Donald's office, slammed the door and walked away still holding the door handle.'

I chuckled, raised my eyebrows and shook my head. Gill had been a few years ahead of me at vet school and fate threw her something of a lemon in this, her first job after graduation. She asked how my morning at Linton had gone and I told her about my embarrassment.

'Sounds like Donald,' she commiserated. 'Never mind. Come and watch me do the afternoon consultations.'

I enjoyed observing how Gill's interaction with pet owners contrasted with that of Donald's. While Gill asked questions about their dogs and cats with a patient solicitousness, Donald's approach had the high-handedness of Vlad the Impaler. Yet, curiously, some of his clients seemed to like this, as if it endowed him with a more assured knowledge and reliability.

Afterwards, Gill and I sat down with a cup of tea while she explained to me her management of a dog with epilepsy. Donald thundered up the corridor and strode into the office.

'Gill,' he instructed after declining our offer of tea, 'there's a pony requiring vaccination in Auborn. Do that, please, on your way home. Don't take Sheilagh: while one young lady is acceptable, two may seem like a Sunday school picnic.'

Gill glanced at me, smiled then nodded before getting up to prepare for her unexpected call.

'Sheilagh,' Donald continued, 'there's a horse you'll be interested in seeing on the way back to Haddington tonight.'

As Donald drove, he tested what I had learned at the stud farm.

'Describe the Caslick's procedure.'

'It's the insertion of stitches in the vulva of a mare,' I answered.

'Indication.'

'To prevent the entry of pathogens, infection and reproductive loss.'

'Timing.'

'After service. Stitches are removed a few days before anticipated foaling.'

Donald nodded, the only manifestation of my correct answers to his questions. But I was pleased with my progress and appreciated that much of this was down to his teaching skills.

He pulled up at a pedestrian crossing on the outskirts of Lincoln and exhaled through his nostrils like a Friesian bull. A frail lady looked at us from the pavement then trembled across the road, one woollen-clad spindle after the other.

'Wouldn't run these legs another season, would you?' Donald sneered.

I had no idea how to respond to this unkindness other than with an awkward smile. We travelled into the open Lincolnshire countryside with large patches of brilliant yellow where oilseed rape grew, lifting my mood. Donald pulled up beside a field with two horses.

'Come and see Merlin,' he said, stepping out of his Subaru estate, as slighted and insulted as the women around him. His rangy frame was clothed in fawn moleskins and a checked cotton shirt, inside which he'd tucked the end of his striped tie, probably to keep it uncontaminated with the fluids and faecal matter exuding from his patients. In the whole four weeks I spent with him, I never saw his brown brogues dirty.

I followed him over a wooden gate and into the field.

'Stand here and watch the chestnut,' he said, approaching the horses. They cantered around the field in response to Donald's shouts and arm waving.

'What do you see, Sheilagh?'

I studied the chestnut as Donald made him move.

'He's stiff on the hind legs,' I answered.

Donald returned, barely breathless, and stood beside me. 'Merlin is a 16-year-old hunter and has shown increasing hind-leg stiffness over the last six months. What are the possibilities?'

'Back problems?'

'Watch again.'

Donald made his way towards the horses then made them run and turn to the left then right.

I looked more closely at the chestnut's movement. The penny dropped.

'Spavin,' I shouted.

'He has bone spavin,' Donald nodded.

I appreciated the efforts he made to help me learn. He rubbed his shoes over some grass and we returned to the car.

A few minutes of driving in silence was broken by Donald cantillating with a priestly fervour, '"*When chapmen billies leave the street and drouthy neighbours, neighbours meet*".'

He glanced at me. 'Can you continue, Sheilagh?'

'Is that a poem?' I asked.

'Indeed. Tam O' Shanter.'

'Robert Burns,' I was relieved I knew, 'but I don't remember it.'

'"*As market days are wearing late and folk begin to tak the gate...*" ' Donald continued to boast his literary knowledge, propounding in his Inverness accent, '"*while we sit bousing at the nappy and getting fou and unco happy...*",' Donald broke his recital, 'love that phrase, "*fou and unco happy*",' he smiled to himself, shook his head and continued, '"*we think na on the lang Scots miles...*".'

I was impressed, but I had hoped for a discussion on the causes, treatments, management and prognosis of bone spavin.

By the end of the poem we had reached Haddington. A lady, whom I recognised as his neighbour, was standing outside Donald's house.

'Oh, Donald, I am sorry. So, so sorry,' she wailed, clutching her wet face then rubbing red eyes. Donald wound down the window.

'Frances, what have you done?' he said with the tone of a policeman to an errant drunkard.

I got out the car and walked round to her.

'I…I…I ran over your cat. Oooh,' Frances's wails were getting louder, 'he dashed out in front of me. I think he's dead, Donald. Dead.'

'Which cat?' Donald asked, apparently unmoved by this terrible news.

'Logie,' she sniffed.

'The ginger one?' Donald frowned.

'Yes,' wailed Francis.

'Oh good,' Donald replied, 'I didn't like him.'

Frances and I stared at Donald, then at each other, but he continued, 'Miss Nisbet will examine the cat to confirm you have killed him.'

Frances howled even louder than before then took me over to the roadside where a ginger body lay motionless. His eyes had glazed over and blood dripped from his ears but I took my stethoscope from my pocket and listened for a heartbeat. After a respectful length of time, I shook my head and removed my stethoscope.

'I'm sorry, Frances,' I said through her sobs. 'It would have been quick, though. He wouldn't have suffered.'

Wendy, Donald's wife, came running out of the house

with a blanket. She gave Frances a hug, then together we wrapped up Logie as we would a crystal vase, ready to lay him to rest.

I took the brief walk to the Old Rectory where I was lodging with Patty and Christopher Jones. Many of the rooms in this Victorian ruin were unusable: filigree carpeting was covered in bits of plaster, wallpaper peeled like sunburned skin and holes in the ceilings made them look like a colander. The smell reminded me of the leaky flat I once had in Glasgow's Maryhill.

I went into the sitting room and saw Christopher in a disintegrating armchair, reading one of his leather-bound volumes. He looked up over his reading glasses and smiled.

I smiled back. 'Interesting book?' I asked, unsure that he would welcome conversation.

He raised his eyebrows and nodded. 'It's about York Minster. Not a blockbuster,' he said, impassively, and returned to reading.

Christopher was a historian who communicated with head movements and facial expressions. I could have counted on my fingers and toes the words I heard him speak during my entire stay. A Doric column of a man, he wore tweed suits that, he told me, had belonged to his grandfather; the trousers were too short and he tried to cover this up by wearing ankle boots. His shirts were worn to the extent that you could see through them and the cuffs were so frayed they resembled fringing.

I found another armchair and took out my notebook and pen from my jacket pocket to write up the cases I'd seen that day. The clock on the oak mantle piece added a liquid rhythm to the amicable silence and faded pink velvet curtains dragged a rectangle of early evening sunlight from the French windows onto brown-stained floor boards. My notes flowed.

The peace was broken with footsteps on the hall flag stones. Patty put her head around the door then stepped in. 'Hello, Sheilagh, didn't hear you come back.'

Patty had a round face, cheeks like plums and pale blue eyes. Feral blonde curls fell to her fulsome bosom, peeking from the top of her T shirt which strained over a well-nourished stomach and met the top of a cheesecloth skirt. Her feet were bare except for red nail varnish on each of her tiny round toe nails. She flounced down on a chair next to me and I smelled a joss stick spiciness.

'Good day with Donald?' she smiled, oozing warmth.

I told her about Merlin and Logie, but didn't mention my humiliation at Linton.

'How was your day?' I asked.

'Okay. Steve, a neighbour, is coming round with things for supper, so he's given me a night off. He owns the knacker's yard up the road.'

'Pullen's?' I asked, 'I've heard mention of him.'

'That's him. Made a lot of money out of it,' Patty commented as she got up. 'Nice evening for a walk around the garden before supper, if you fancy.'

We walked together, Patty still in her bare feet. She was one of the few people I had felt at ease with from the moment we met and I felt drawn to her self-effacing honesty. The garden covered about two acres and surrounded the house, and its aroma reflected a high summer verdancy with top notes of honeysuckle. There were low crumbling walls covered in grey and yellow lichen and the cobbled paths were carpeted with moss. Patty chatted about their son, Richard, who was at Harrow school.

'With his grandmother's, Christopher's mother, support,' she added.

I was bewildered that she confided this to me, an almost stranger.

'Is he happy there?' I asked.

'He is now, yes,' she smiled, and didn't elaborate.

Scrunching gravel heralded Steve's arrival. We joined him as he took a crate of Bollinger and a bag with two entire beef fillet muscles from the back of his Range Rover into the kitchen. I had never seen this meat in its entirety before and I stared at the torpedo-shaped tumescence, seeping blood like pomegranate juice onto the worktop surface. Patty cut the fillets into steaks and asked Steve to open one of the bottles.

'Try it, Sheilagh,' she urged as Steve handed me a tumbler of the fizzing, clear, straw-coloured liquid.

I hadn't drunk champagne before so the taste was wasted on me, but I took a sip. The bubbles exploding on my tongue reminded me of a sherbet fountain with a bitter aftertaste instead of liquorice.

The other two lodgers joined us. Martin was tall with greasy black hair and the sort of profile that made him hard to see when he stood sideways. He was an administrative assistant in a lawyer's office and seemed to fancy Jackie, a groom in a nearby riding school. Jackie's hair was Barbie doll big, and I wondered how she fitted it into her riding hat. Her bottom and thighs seemed to have a similar struggle with the jodhpurs she appeared never to remove.

More people arrived and Patty introduced us. After a second tumbler of Bollinger, it seemed as if I'd known them all for years and I felt like Tam O' Shanter.

'The steak was lovely,' I said to Patty later as we cleared up, 'and I hadn't seen one bottle of Bollinger before never mind a crate.'

She handed me an empty. 'Take this as a memento,' then added, 'Steve is good to us.'

'Yes,' I said, accepting the green bottle, 'two whole fillets.'

'We never enquire after the provenance of Steve's gifts, however,' Christopher commented, filling the dishwasher.

I shared a smile with Christopher, enjoying his sense of the absurd.

The next morning, with a feeling of other-worldliness and soft ringing in my ears, both unfamiliar to me, I joined Donald at the Linton Stud to complete passports for young stock to be exported. I was relieved that the grooms who had drawn so much amusement from my last visit were not around.

'There's a mare to be covered this afternoon, Miss Nisbet,' Donald said as he supervised me vaccinating a foal, 'but I have asked Tony to bring it forward to this morning so you can see it.'

Tony, the yard manager, nodded.

'Thank you. I look forward to that,' I said making eye contact with both Donald and Tony. I was touched by Donald's determination to ensure I saw as much as possible.

As we watched the covering, Donald explained in detail the purpose of each of the steps.

'The mare is booted,' he said, pointing to the felted boots on the horse's hind feet. 'On account of the stallion's value, managerial precautions must be taken to prevent his injury,' Donald continued as if reading from a textbook.

He glanced at me. I nodded. He went on.

'Reciprocally, the leather collar around the mare's neck is there to protect her from the stallion's teeth.'

'Seems only fair,' I answered, 'even though her value is likely to be a fraction of the stallion's.'

Donald raised a non-committal eyebrow.

Tony wrapped a bandage around the mare's tail then, lifting a bucket of soapy water, washed around her tail head and hind legs. I recognised the groom who led in the stallion as one of the smirkers on my last visit. He walked on the left hand side of the horse, which was bouncing off the ground as if on springs. The stallion arched his neck and pulled away from the groom, knocking him off balance.

'What do you call that behaviour?' Donald asked me, when the stallion lifted his upper lip and sniffed.

'Incompetent?' I suggested as the groom found his feet again.

Donald glanced at me. 'Sarcasm, Sheilagh, does not become you,' he said with the tone that Mrs Bennett might have used to her daughter Elizabeth. 'I think you know I referred to the stallion's facial posture.'

When he'd regained control of his charge, the groom noticed me at the side of the yard. I smiled sweetly. He turned a delightful red.

'Flehmen,' I said, turning to Donald. 'It's thought to help the stallion detect the mare's hormones.'

Donald nodded. As Tony took the stallion's lead rope and led him to the mare to complete this most fundamental procedure, I realised that I was gaining a considerable knowledge of human behaviour besides equine medicine.

Afterwards, we bought sandwiches at a nearby shop and ate them during the drive back to the surgery. When he had finished eating, Donald patted his mouth with a spotless and neatly-folded white cotton handkerchief that he'd taken from his trouser pocket then glanced at me.

'Sheilagh,' he said, 'would you like to come back for the first week in September?'

Never, not ever, had I been invited back to a practice. I had got on well with all of them, and their reports prepared for the vet school were favourable, but no one had indicated that they'd like me to return. The inference that Donald had a high regard for me brought a light-headedness to equal that incurred by Steve's Bollinger. Donald would rather have me back to see practice than offer an opportunity to any other vet student. What approval. What overt, incontrovertible endorsement of my abilities and potential.

I gulped a mouthful of ham and bread. 'Yes, I would. Very much.'

'Good,' Donald smiled, sweeping a crumb from his lap. 'You see, it's the equine veterinary conference in Dublin then and I'd like to take Wendy – it will be a break for her – and we would be pleased if you would look after the children.'

I looked at the remains of my sandwich. How could he? He had taken me skydiving then thrown me out without a parachute. Look after his kids, for goodness sake. My light-headedness hit earth with a sledgehammer thump.

'Sheilagh?'

I couldn't sum up any excuse. I was cornered.

Seething and rankling, I recovered enough to say. 'Yes, of course. I haven't spent much time with children recently, but I'm sure that will be fine.'

'Good. You can chat with Wendy later over the details,' he smiled.

Still brooding over this, I returned to the Old Rectory that evening.

'Everything okay, Sheilagh?' Patty asked.

I was sitting in the kitchen watching her prepare supper. She mashed a cauldron of potatoes, the flesh at the back of her bare arms wobbling with every blow, her lips pursed with each downward thud. She tapped the masher against the side of the pot then, with a huge tarnished spoon, spread the mash in fluffy lumps onto a carpet of mince.

I told her about Donald's duplicity.

'Hmm. I see why you're disappointed.'

She turned to me and smiled then opened the AGA door and placed the dish of Shepherd's pie inside. With a torn blue gingham dish cloth, she rubbed her hands then walked over to give me a hug.

'But I suppose it's a compliment that he'd like you take care of his family – and you can come round and see us, too,' she said.

I nodded, accepting the anodynes of her words and friendship.

Towards the end of my stay, Donald took Wendy and their three young children, Colin, Morag and Peter, away for a long weekend and asked me to call round before they left.

'Ah, Sheilagh, I'm going to show you what to do while we are away,' he advised.

This was not a request. This was a list of duties expected of me. Each evening I was required to fill two bowls with dried *Go Cat* for the remaining cats, John and Baird, then water the potatoes and greenhouse vegetables. I then had to collect some sweet peas, empty then re-fill the flower jars in the house, then take the post from behind the door and put it on the kitchen table. My next duty was to walk Brian, the tri-coloured collie, and feed him his *Chappie*, repeating this each morning.

'Twice daily, Sheilagh, morning and evening,' Donald continued with a degree of pedantry, 'you must attach the hose to the tap in the garage then fill up Arkle's water bucket.'

I frowned, wondering why a Cheltenham Gold Cup winner, a dead one indeed, had ended up in a Haddington paddock.

'Morag's Highland pony,' Donald explained, as he led me to the garage to show me the location of the tap. 'In return,' Donald finished with magnanimity, 'you may read the textbooks in my study. Note the questions you have for me on my return.'

I swallowed my resentment and mustered sufficient grace to thank him and wish him a good holiday.

The next evening after finishing my chores and picking up and bagging the dog poo as well, I looked through Donald's books. Taking them out from the book case, one by one, I saw that each of the fatigued and frayed veterinary tomes had on the first page a list of former owners whose names were written in various styles of cursive hand writing and all crossed out and footed with the bold, black inked and capitalised final owner, 'D.G. FRASER'.

The pages of one book were the colour of channel island cream, just as thick and with a rough texture. Page after page of print in a tiny-sized font was relieved with occasional drawings. Some were of dissection specimens and had arrows beginning in a muscle or tendon or bone and ending in a name in italicized Latin. Many of the pages were annotated on the margins with notes or aide memoirs like 'c.f. antebrachium p.459' or 'NB for exam' or 'discuss with Prof T'. It all looked so arcane, so obscure, as if I'd wondered into the classical studies section of a library by mistake.

And then, tucked between Blood and Henderson's *Veterinary Medicine* and a March 1961 copy of *The Veterinary Record,* I found Donald's lecture notes, still in flawless condition after twenty years. The unlined pages of the hardback notebook, about A4 size, were covered in Donald's crowded writing, some of which he had written in short hand. It hadn't occurred to me to do that and even if it had, I doubt I'd have found the time to learn shorthand at the same time as negotiating my way through the long and intensive veterinary course. But Donald clearly had. His resourcefulness, inspiration and sagacity left me awestruck.

I sat down with Brian next to the window overlooking the fecund garden and the paddock at the bottom with the round-bellied Arkle. The church clock chimed eight times into the melodious village serenity. The sweet peas' fragrance complemented the tranquility of the house and the evening was warm. I opened Adams *Lameness in Horses* and realised that, with Donald's thorny yet bountiful encouragement, I was on my way to being what I'd always wanted to be.

5

Adaptation

'It is not the most intellectual of the species that survives; it is not the strongest that survives; but the species that survives is the one that is able to adapt to the changing environment in which it finds itself.'

CHARLES DARWIN

I had little idea of what roles vets may fill when I graduated and, like most of my peers, viewed my career through the tunnel that ended in general practice. Of the Glasgow graduates of my late seventies vintage, most of us went into practice, a few started post-graduate degrees and one or two of the girls got married and never lifted a syringe again in their lives.

A pilaster of a man from the Royal Army Veterinary Corps had attempted to seduce us in final year into fighting for Queen and Country while enjoying responsibility for the British Army's dogs and horses. The captain delivered his pitch as if we all wore hearing aids and with a pedantic enunciation more suited to an audience whose first language is not English. He included details on the good level of pay, travel to exotic places, excellent career prospects and supportive camaraderie. But the six-week induction at Sandhurst with reveille at five a.m. and training regimes that would make labouring on the Burma railway seem like a team away day induced only one of us to take the Queen's Shilling. It wasn't long before Chris was promoted to Major, had been on manoeuvres in several countries and you could balance a cup and saucer in the right angle between the base of his spine and his buttocks.

Then there was the semi-comatose soul from the Ministry of Agriculture, his skin as grey as what was left of his hair, who described, with the enthusiasm I'd seen in lambs about to become chops, his work in controlling notifiable diseases like tuberculosis and brucellosis in cattle.

'Each cow is contained safely within the confines of a sturdy crush before the neck is shaved then, after the skin thickness is measured and the measurements carefully noted, tuberculin is given intra-dermally,' he droned in a voice as resigned as it was passive. How we wished for hearing aids we could take out that afternoon.

Joan Robinson, a professor in the surgery department, had suggested I go on to study for a master of veterinary medicine degree and while I was chuffed to be asked, I needed a break from studying and research. So, as a compromise, I decided I'd be a house surgeon for a year which would keep my foot in the camp of academia while starting to practise the theory I had worked so hard to learn. I was offered a post in one of the other vet schools but as this didn't start until the October after I graduated, I looked for a locum position.

Jim Harte, a gently-spoken man with understated kindliness from Sallins, County Kildare welcomed me to his Gainsborough practice two weeks after I graduated and was admitted to the Royal College of Veterinary Surgeons. He offered guidance without bossing me; gave me enough rope but not enough to hang from. When I needed help, he was there; if I wanted to work it out myself, he left me to it.

What helped me settle so well were the friends I made in his wife, Betty, and their children, John and Rachel. Betty was the only child of Cambridgeshire arable farmers. Besides the differences in our respective age, Betty seemed to have enjoyed a more comfortable upbringing than I had: she spent school holidays in hotels whereas my parents took me camping; for every Michelin-starred meal Betty enjoyed I was marched up Arthur's Seat for a picnic. Nonetheless, we became friends and I enjoyed her company.

When I'd finished my first evening surgery Betty invited me in to the house.

'John,' she said to her son, who was around my age, 'would you go to the off-licence and get a bottle of Dom Perignon. Get the rosé one. Jim's on call, isn't he, Sheilagh,' she said turning to me, 'so you and I can enjoy a drink together, if you'd like.'

Her brown eyes sparkled as she fluttered into an armchair and smoothed down her shoulder-length brunette hair before waving to me to join her. When we knew each other better, she admitted that she didn't actually know what natural colour her hair was, as she had her roots done every week.

I was taken aback with the warmth of her gesture; her unmistakable offer of friendship. I walked into her sitting room from the hallway that throughout my time with the practice bore the delicate fragrances of whichever Crabtree and Evelyn soap she had placed in the bathroom's hand basin. I could feel my feet being engulfed by the carpet and when I sat down in an armchair it was several seconds before I stopped sinking. There were floor to ceiling curtains, held back with shiny cord ties and a collection of Royal Doulton on a mahogany table. Photographs in silver or wooden frames of babies, children, older people, dogs and horses posing beautifully for the camera, were on every flat surface.

When John returned, the three of us drank the champagne, Betty and I doing most of the talking. I can't remember what we talked about but we didn't run out of things to say. I wasn't only her husband's new temporary assistant; I was becoming her confidante.

I worked hard, made many friends and more than a few mistakes; rejoiced with my successes. John helped me fill my weekends off with jaunts to Clumber Park and Chatsworth, walks in the Peak District and a visit to Claxby to prove that Lincolnshire wasn't entirely on a flat plain. When I hear now of the dire, dispiriting, the downright dissillusioning starts that some new veterinary graduates have, starts that are sufficient to have them leave the profession a few years later, I realise the extent to which I landed on my feet with Jim Harte.

'Would you like to stay with us?' Jim asked me towards the end of my locum and as I was preparing in my mind to become a house surgeon. I found it difficult to refuse this offer from people who had been so kind, who had welcomed me into, and treated me as one of, their family.

The forty weeks of extra-mural studies I completed as an undergraduate had adjusted my expectations of general veterinary practice and I knew, of course, that Herriot-esque imaginings of spending hour after blissful hour alleviating pain and suffering and becoming the apotheosis of benevolence towards animals were unrealistic. But I had gone into it unaware that lurking in the small print for my profession was this: being a vet is not as much about working with animals as it is about working with the people who work with, or keep, animals. And I found this epiphany as cataclysmic as ordering the T-bone and getting nut cutlet.

General veterinary practice requires the diplomacy of Ghandi, the wisdom of the Dalai Lama, and the tenacity of spring-grass cow poo for byre walls. Enabling people to understand what you believe is wrong with their animals and what you propose to do about it are just as important as clinical and diagnostic skills. You need the tact, firmness and foresight of history's most gifted and inspirational leaders. You need sufficient empathy to appreciate why a dog you see late on a Friday evening owned by a woman with three toddlers and a baby in a buggy was not brought to you as early as it should have been. But most of all you need to like people, all sorts of people, as much as you like their animals.

It wasn't that I didn't feel able to do as well as most vets in meeting these requirements. In fact now, nearly forty years on, having endured a number of life's hardest challenges and been blessed with its most joyous times, I believe I would find the 'people' side of practice more easy. But it wasn't what I had signed up for in choosing to study veterinary medicine. So I declined Jim's offer. Jim and Betty have now both passed away, but one legacy of my brief time with them is the life-long friend I made in their son, John, whose unconventional sentiments and shrewd perspicacities often feel like a whack on the side of my head.

I've always loved making things. Like turning a lump of clay into a mug or egg cup. Or creating an ornament from bits of cloth, wool and buttons. Or taking damaged clothes and sewing and re-shaping until they're wearable again. So it was no surprise that I enjoyed small animal operating so much, away from the circumspect gaze of owners and within the tranquility of theatre. Even now, the smell of Hibiscrub, the luscious pink soap we used for scrubbing up, transports me back to theatre and I miss the soothing, plopping rhythm and whooshing exhalations of the anaesthetic machines.

As a house surgeon, nothing gave me more delight than a weekend on call repairing fractures, stitching up wounds and doing emergency hysterectomies. My first ever working Christmas day got off to a start with a Pekingese whose left eye was dangling out of its socket.

'This is Midge,' the owner said, his stripy pyjama top peaking over his sweatshirt. 'It happened after he snatched and ran off with the pigs in blankets.'

He handed the flat-faced pooch to me for admission to theatre, replacement of his swinging eye then stitching over his eyelids.

'Nice to have a tall house surgeon for a change,' remarked Mr Sands the following New Year, as he used the foot lever to elevate the operating table to a height comfortable for him and adjusted his face mask to cover his sparse black beard – it may well have been he who made stubble a desirable fashion accessory – while the veterinary nurses prepared a Dachshund for surgery. Mr Sands was known for his expertise in, amongst other orthopaedic procedures, the surgical treatment of herniated intervertebral discs, a problem in particular in long-backed dogs with short limbs. He was also known for his intransigence regarding phone messages while he was operating and the surgical secretary, Janet, knew never to disturb him, whatever the degree of apparent urgency.

Mr Sands was about half an hour into the Dachshund's operation when Janet tapped on the window between theatre and the hallway. I looked up. Mr Sands ignored her. Janet beckoned to me and showed me a note she'd written. I went over to the window and read, 'Tell Mr Sands a man about a book is on the phone.'

I mouthed 'no way'.

Janet scribbled again and held up the paper, 'he says Mr Sands will surely speak to him.'

I frowned but nodded and went back to the operating table.

'Um, Mr Sands,' I began.

'What?' he barked, as he parted the muscles along the dog's spinal column and picked up some retractors.

'Well, we don't want to disturb you but Janet says there's a gentleman on the phone for you. He says he'd like to speak to you about a book and he feels sure you'll want to know he's ...'

'Take these,' he said, handing me the retractors, 'position them correctly and consider what we will do next. I'll be back in a minute.'

Beneath the mask, my mouth was wide open as I watched Mr Sands take off his gown and gloves and walk out of theatre. The nurses and I stared at each other, eyes like dinner plates at this unprecedented behaviour. When he returned, re-gloved and re-gowned he continued the procedure on the dog as if he'd done nothing unusual.

'What was the book, Janet?' I asked when I'd removed my scrubs and got dressed again later that afternoon. 'Is it the one on spinal surgery Mr Sands is writing?'

Janet shook her head, smiled and bent her head towards me. 'It's one about sailing in Sardinia,' she whispered.

'Sailing? In Sardinia?' I whispered back, my eyebrows reaching the ceiling.

Janet nodded and put her hand over her mouth to stifle a giggle.

I enjoyed the aura in this veterinary school; it felt

different to the one in Glasgow where the zeal to push back the frontiers of veterinary medicine initiated by senior staff was contracted by junior staff who then re-ignited the senior staff and on and up in a giddy spiral of clinical and surgical excellence. Jostling for supremacy was assisted by getting your papers published but not just in any journal; it had to be one with a high impact factor – the measure of how often the journal's articles have been cited over a stated time.

It wasn't that the surgeons I worked for didn't work hard: they, too, produced much influential work. But in contrast to Glasgow, the surgery department of my postgraduate role was not only a forum for the exchange of ground-breaking ideas and information but one that also left room for elements of the gentlemen's club; attitudes were humane and well-grounded; aware that life was short.

Of course, the difference in how I felt about the two schools may be explained by my differing status at each of them, undergraduate in one and junior member of staff in the other. However, the senior surgeons I worked with, as well as showing me how important hobbies were to mental and physical health, created an environment that allowed me to build on the knowledge I gained in Glasgow and when my year's tenure came to an end, I was sorry to leave.

A brief wrong turn into more general practice followed. I think this was because at that time I could not cure myself of the insidious and widely-held standpoint that this was the only province for 'real' vets; to do anything else marked you as invertebrate, lily-livered and unable to withstand the rigours of frontline veterinary medicine. To do anything else was regarded as less of a career choice than Hobson's choice, something to resort to if the strength of your body or mind did not reach that of colleagues who had stayed in practice. So it took a while for me to challenge the prevailing rhetoric and explore what else I could do with an MRCVS.

Besides the limitations of general practice I'd already learned, I discovered how little of the the vast knowledge you gather as a vet student you put into regular use. The implications of the maxim 'common things are common' weighed on me like a weekend weather forecast of persistent rain and I mourned the relative infrequency of suspect diabetics, Cushing's disease and other more challenging cases.

'You could look into the Ministry,' Alan, a colleague I met at a local veterinary meeting, suggested.

I screwed up my eyes and clenched my jaws together, remembering the 'Mr Grey' who spoke to us in final year. 'Isn't lobotomy a compulsory requirement for that?' I asked.

Alan smiled. 'Actually, my wife has just joined up.'

I inhaled deeply. 'Alan, I'm sorry to offend.'

He shook his head. 'Linda would find that funny and, you know, she may have the last laugh. It's early days, but she certainly appreciates the shorter working hours with negligible on call and she doesn't miss one tiny bit the practice daily diet of dogs with itchy skins, sore ears, diarrhoea and blocked anal glands.'

All this struck not just a chord with me but a whole symphony. I needed to find out more.

Alan gave me some names and I went along to see my local Divisional Veterinary Officer. A pleasant and welcoming man – and a peer of the 'Mr Grey' of my final year lecture – he spent time explaining to me the range of duties Veterinary Officers do to control notifiable diseases, support trade in animals and their products, and keep standards of animal welfare high. This seemed a much more interesting and varied job than I'd hitherto believed, but it was a visit to my nearest Veterinary Investigation Service laboratory that began my new career trajectory.

When I arrived at the lab to have a look around, I was welcomed by the ambience of that morning's post mortems on sheep that must have been several days dead. The stench of putrefaction, rumen contents and faeces filled the air and I was surprised to see the receptionist tucking into a packet of crisps as he slid back the glass window to greet me.

'Hulloo,' he said through a mouthful of cheese and onion.

I introduced myself, noticing a Tupperware lunch box placed not far from a clear bag with an opaque yellow liquid labelled 'calf diarrhoea sample' and a small bottle of tapeworms swimming around in gut contents.

'Ah, Sheilagh, nice to meet you. I'm Mike,' he said, and nodded his head, sparsely covered with strands of hair that made it look like pampas grass. 'Mr Reid said to let him know when you arrived. Hang on, I'll give him a call.'

Soon, coming up the corridor I saw a thin, middle-aged gentleman whose hair and lab coat were both thick and white, but only the latter reached below his knees. His front teeth had the angle of Bugs Bunny's and the skin on his neck reminded me of the tortoise I'd had when I was a student. With him was an older lady wearing a woollen hat to which was pinned a badge with the 'ban the bomb' logo. She wore a long tweed skirt, white ankle socks and flat, black lace up shoes.

'Sheilagh,' the gentleman said to me as he approached. 'I'm Jock Reid, senior veterinary investigation officer, and this is Felicity Granger, one of my VIOs.

I shook hands with them both.

'Felicity has kindly agreed to show you some of the lab, Sheilagh, then you can come back to see me for a wee chat, if you'd like.'

'I'll look forward to that,' I said and turning to the lady added, 'thank you, Mrs Granger.'

'Miss,' she replied. 'But call me Felicity. I'll get you a lab coat and we'll start in parasitology.'

We walked into a high-ceilinged room with white-tiled walls from top to bottom. Large tin-surrounded light bulbs dangled from long cords from the ceiling and I shivered in the remorseless chill. Felicity led me over to a series of large Belfast stone sinks, where a woman in the *de rigueur* white lab coat and bright yellow gloves was manipulating a tagliatelle of intestines.

'Jill,' Felicity began, 'this is Sheilagh. She's in practice just now but thinking of joining us in the VI Service.'

We exchanged hi's and smiles before Jill returned to her Italianate task.

'Jill is preparing a total worm count on this material from a three month old lamb. What might we expect?'

Felicity gave me an expressionless look. I did a mental gallop through my third year parasitology notes.

I had a stab at it. 'Nematodirus?'

The smell of decaying gut contents filled my nostrils and made my stomach star jump against my diaphragm. Jill and Felicity seemed unaffected.

'I agree, yes,' I was relieved to obtain Felicity's approval. 'Note how Jill is washing out the entire gut. She'll collect the washings in a bucket before taking a sample for analysis.'

'I can see tapeworms, too,' I said.

'Yup. Already sampled a few of those,' Jill said to Felicity. 'Going to Weybridge for identification.'

Felicity nodded. 'Good work, Jill. Make sure you have time for your lunch.'

'Will do. I'm starving. Looking forward to my bolognese.'

'Nice,' Felicity said. My stomach heaved. 'Biochemistry next, Sheilagh.'

We walked down a long corridor lined with display cabinets. Perspex boxes containing mounted specimens swimming in formalin filled the cream-coloured shelves. There were pigs' feet with oval-shaped ulcers, a cow's tongue with large blisters and a bull's penis on the end of which was a wart-like growth the size of a cauliflower.

'How long have you been a VIO, Felicity?' I asked.

Her woolly hat was now in the pocket of her lab coat to expose her grey hair scraped back into a bun at the nape of her neck. A brown plastic alice band ensured that not one hair strand was tempted to break ranks.

'Thirty odd years. Best job I've done. Bovine infertility is my main interest. Fascinating. How long have you been qualified?'

'A couple of years. About half of it in practice,' I replied.

'A good start. But wise to look around, too.'

We walked into another white-tiled room with dark brown floor boards. There were large machines coughing out bits of paper and desktop ones spinning round like a washing machine.

'Biochemistry,' Felicity announced.

'Smells sweeter than parasitology,' I said.

Felicity stopped and turned round to look at me. 'Smell? We don't complain about that, Sheilagh. Smell is an important diagnostic tool,' she lowered her head while still eye-balling me, then continued. 'When you can smell dysentery before you see it, you're beginning to become a clinician.'

I nodded obediently, and followed behind her as she swept around the labs, her flat shoes making swooshing sounds on the floorboards.

'What? You want to do what?' replied Professor Robinson when I asked her for a reference in my application to join the Ministry of Agriculture, Fisheries and Food's Veterinary Investigation Service. 'You're a practitioner to your finger tips, Sheilagh. You know working for MAFF entails long periods of boredom interrupted by bouts of panic,' she finished, paraphrasing epigrams about conditions in First World War trenches.

But I wasn't put off.

Three months later I stood in Jock's lab as a newly-appointed VIO with an equally new lab coat that reached my shins, like the hand-me-down school coats I wore and never grew into. Once my induction was completed, watching and assisting the experienced VIOs, it was good to have the post-mortem room to myself. I stood alone, other than with the hapless animals on the aluminium table before me, the place offering the peace and total absorption in my work that I enjoyed when operating.

How germs work inside animals is fascinating. Each one carries out its damaging business in different ways, spreading from where it first got into the animal's body via the bloodstream to more distant parts. The parts favoured by particular bacteria or viruses varies, so that some streptococcal bacteria head for a lamb's limb joints, for example, while other bacteria prefer the lungs. Then those that don't need oxygen to grow and multiply, flourish in the dark recesses of muscle tissues. It's horses for courses, in the same way that some of us choose Benidorm for our summer holidays while others couldn't be happier anywhere than up Cairngorm.

Then when the wee nasties arrive at their destination, the trouble starts. Sometimes, they excrete toxins that damage the animals' cells causing small haemorrhages. Cells in the animals' blood attack and kill the bacteria, creating the yellowish-white mucousy stuff we call pus.

Animal disease, and all the factors that play a role in making it happen, is a fascinating study and I loved my time as a pathologist. Working out which disease or condition an animal had died of, why, and what needed to be done to stop it happening to other animals, was as intriguing and absorbing as unravelling the murderer and their evil means was for Hercule Poirot.

But, as Poirot may have himself pointed out, tout passe, tout casse, tout lasse. And this proverb meaning everything passes, everything breaks, everything becomes wearisome, was evidently interpreted by Thatcher's government as a requirement to reduce public spending by, amongst other things, closing the government-run laboratory where I worked.

'We'll start you off, Sheilagh,' Dougal, my new boss, said on my first morning in my new role as a field veterinary officer with MAFF, 'by asking you to help John with sheep diseases and Sarah with TB.'

My smiles and keen nods belied the descent of my heart to my Doc Martens. I was missing my VIO role already, but for various reasons it made sense to accept the offer of a job not far from where my lab had been. The field role was meaningful and relevant, of course, but its standardised, regulated-to-a-breath nature seemed to differ from the observational, investigative and intuitive skills required of a pathologist.

But I hunkered down, grew in confidence with the work, escaped for a while to the pig industry, returned with renewed interest, and I was grateful to find that the only thing Sarah had in common with 'Mr Grey' was an expertise in bovine tuberculosis. BSE in cattle was still abundant and I enjoyed becoming more skilled in the early recognition of the disease. Advising and helping farmers whose animals had been the subjects of welfare concerns to take better care of their livestock also gave me a sense of achievement and I enjoyed the challenges of outbreaks of notifiable disease. Much of my work was invigorating intellectually, within a supportive environment and I availed myself of the numerous courses offered to staff, from firearms training to public speaking and IT to increasing personal resilience, and collaborated with diverse groups of people. And all through this, I was indebted to Dougal's leadership, fine-grained with elements of the frivolous.

'So, let's take a look at our new orgasmogram,' he said, expressionless, during an afternoon team meeting, while adjusting the half-rims providing a contradictory air of wisdom and authority, and clicking the mouse to move to the next PowerPoint slide.

With most of the meeting, I smiled at his play on words, a skittish poke in the ribs of late twentieth century corporate decorum and political correctness.

Dougal's wit made meetings, like channel island cream to your porridge, palatable. His satirical approach to some of our procedures, like the 'too difficult' tray he proposed he should have on his desk in between the trays marked 'in' and 'out', and his rubber stamp to mark documents for his attention with 'I am too busy to read this rubbish', also drew chuckles from even the hardest-nosed civil servants. But he ran a tight ship and I came to know the importance of remaining agile enough to ask, whenever he said jump, 'how high?' on the way up. He made sure his team met all its requirements and he encouraged us to widen our skills and develop our government careers.

The organogram of our organisation appeared on the screen behind Dougal. Senior figures were at the top, the lowest ranked staff at the bottom. The diagram identified the seniors by name and the lower ranks by job title only, and Dougal cheered us by commenting that an alternative arrangement for an organogram was the one like a flower pot, with all the hoi-polloi as the bright and fragrant flowers and the seniors as the manure at the bottom of the container.

On another occasion, taking a break from my report of a welfare visit to a flock of store lambs, I picked up my mug containing the dregs of the previous day's Alta Rica and went along to the staff kitchen. The lack of noise for the time of day, mid-morning, surprised me and then I noticed outside the kitchen door a sledgehammer with a post-it note bearing Dougal's handwriting.

'Weapon of mouse destruction,' I read to myself, smiled and opened the door.

Some of my colleagues were standing by the kettle looking as sombre as if they'd received their P45's. I asked what was up.

'Dougal's note. Outside,' Peter answered.

'Oh, I see,' I lied, 'em, what's the story on the mouse?'

'It's only one harmless mouse…,' began Cathy, a vegetarian, although she wore a leather belt.

'But one is sometimes enough to cause trouble,' offered Norma, another meatless eater although I'd known her to succumb to a bacon sandwich.

'Yes, I know, but the humane catcher worked fine,' asserted Cathy, who was said not to like leafy vegetables but would eat pulses.

Norma continued with her legendary diplomacy. 'It didn't get hurt, of course, and we released the mouse in the car park, but the problem was it came back in again.'

My face ached with attempts to keep it straight. The room went silent.

I poured boiling water from the urn onto my coffee granules and tried to think of the right thing to say.

'Well, you know, vermin poisons nowadays are generally considered humane.'

They all seemed to find their shoes fascinating.

'And actually, you know,' I continued, 'one of the recommended means of piglet euthanasia is a sharp blow to its head.'

Cathy picked up her mug, the one with ears for handles and a nose between them and her one-cup-size teapot and stared ahead as she walked passed me towards the door leaving an infusion of contempt and Earl Grey in her wake.

Dougal's office was half way down the corridor on the left-hand side, opposite the poster on how to keep rabies out of the country and another with the contact details for the staff welfare team. He called me in as I passed.

'Did you see my note outside the kitchen?' he smiled, swirling round the last mouthfuls of tea at the bottom of his mug and standing with most of his weight on one foot, while swinging the other foot back and forth, the way he always did when he knew he was a little out of line but considered it safe enough to go ahead anyway.

'Your note … and the response from some of the team,' I frowned at him in mock reprimand.

Dougal shrugged and sat down in one of the comfy chairs next to the low round coffee table in his office, one of the few symbols in the organisation of senior rank. He beckoned me to sit in the chair opposite him.

'What do you think of Adam's new car?' he asked with a frown, so I knew the answer he was hoping for.

'The smart wee Italian coupé with the personalised plate,' I said.

Dougal crossed one leg over the other and swung the foot, flapping the end of his tie against his tummy. 'It's inappropriate for farm visits, don't you think?'

I nodded. 'Might get dirty, I suppose …'

He looked at me, held his head to one side and kept frowning.

'… and perhaps a bit too flashy,' I offered.

'Yes, I thought so, too, and I've had a word with him. He wasn't pleased – worked hard all his life for it, apparently,' Dougal rolled his eyes, 'but he said he would bring his wife's Corsa to work instead.'

I nodded. 'And she gets the coupé?'

'Posh totty, Adam says.'

How very Adam, I thought, as I visualised the fifty something party animal with the roaring voice, seasonal jumpers with dangly bits, and a store of indecent games that he taught us at office Christmas lunches. With nothing more potent than tea and a career's-worth of anecdotes, he brought genuine laughter to the strained jollity and sometimes laboured task of conversation-making amongst people trying to avoid talking shop.

Thirty-six years after I was admitted to the Royal

College of Veterinary Surgeons, I retired from the profession, and during this time, I enjoyed a range of veterinary work in general practice, academia, industry and government as variable as the Scottish weather and as uplifting as a double-shot Americano. Although demanding and requiring long hours, my work allowed me time and energy to bring up a large family and, overall, I reckon I was as fortunate as anyone who has made a living with an MRCVS. But central to it all were the people I worked with and met in the course of my career; human nature in its rich variety, its commonality and diversity, its alliances and altercations and its cohesion through common aims.

Work motivates us, inspires us, feeds and houses us, and passes our time between leaving day-and-night education and growing geraniums. But its fundamental element is the cause it gives us to spend time in the company of other people; people with whom we have a reciprocal shaping, consoling, encouraging and provision of insights into how to adapt, evolve and negotiate a way through life; people with whom we exchange, unwittingly and sublimely, ideas on how to be human.

So here is the exquisite irony: working with people, the fundamental I hadn't signed up for in choosing to become a vet, the very element I had tried to avoid, was what made my work what it was and myself what I became.

6

HENRY'S HEDGES

The door of Gerald's office was closed so I looked through the window in it. Against the wall were two vertical spindles, black hairs protruding at right angles like a loo brush, ending in brown loafers, soles facing the ceiling. Alarmed, I knocked.

'Gerald, are you okay?'

No reply.

'Gerald?'

I opened the door, millimetre at a time. Gerald was standing on his head, his brown woolly jumper covering his eyes and ears, the hems of his trousers around his knees. I waited. Eventually, he lowered his legs and lay prone on the floor and when he saw my feet, raised his head.

'Oh, sorry,' he said getting up and pulling his jumper over his tummy and down to meet his trousers. 'My usual lunchtime routine. Good for the blood pressure.'

Gerald was a veterinary pathologist colleague of mine. In cold weather, he wore a knitted hat complete with pom-pom which sat on his bald head just above his ears so that it didn't get splashed with undesirable fluids while he worked through the decaying remains of farmed livestock accepted for post mortem examination.

Although a large man with a girth that pushed out his vinyl post mortem apron so that it protruded from his waist like a bustle, he was a keen squash player and defeated the most agile opponent simply through his bulky occupation of the court and by ball speeds that would shame a Wimbledon Men's Singles ace.

He was a brilliant clinician and diagnostician with an encyclopaedic knowledge of veterinary medicine. As a relatively new graduate and developing pathologist, I referred to him often for advice, which he gave with patience and enthusiasm. Gerald also had bipolar disorder.

On this occasion, I had decided to ask him about egg peritonitis, which I'd seen amongst a batch of laying hens.

Gerald got up and walked to his desk. He opened the top left drawer, pulled out a raw onion, peeled off the brown skin and bit into it as I would an apple.

'Gerald, that's an onion.'

He nodded. 'Also good for the blood pressure,' he asserted through a full mouth. 'What can I do for you, Sheilagh?'

'Well,' I said, trying to remember. 'Em, I wanted your advice on egg peritonitis, if you wouldn't mind.' I took the seat at the opposite side of the desk. 'It's the birds from the experimental farm again and I'd like to add more to my report that might help them control the problem.'

Gerald nodded, finished his onion, then opened the second drawer of his desk and took out a toothbrush and tube of Colgate.

'Give me a minute,' he said and made his way up to the gents.

'Now, when I was in the middle east,' he began when he returned, exhaling minty-freshness, 'egg peritonitis was largely unrecognised. In fact, I found it difficult to explain to ...'

The phone on Gerald's desk rang. 'Excuse me, Sheilagh,' he said, picking up the receiver. 'Yes?...Goodwin from Southbridge?... Hmm. Tell him I'll ring back in a mo.'

The odours of onion and toothpaste filled Gerald's office and stung my eyes.

'Insufferable man. Do you know him, Sheilagh? Albert Goodwin. Anyway,' Gerald said, with a wink, 'this will prevent further interruptions.'

He picked up two pigeon identity rings and placed one each side of the telephone cradle beneath the receiver. 'So, when switchboard rings,' he chuckled, 'they think the line's engaged, and anyone passing sees the phone has not been left off the hook.'

'Ingenious,' I said, impressed with his mischievous ploy to snatch some time out.

'Hmm. Especially when things get a bit, well, busy,' Gerald confided.

I was fond of Gerald and held him in high regard.

Although he engaged in squash, yoga and healthy eating to enhance his mental health, he controlled his psychological disorder primarily with medication.

Management of mental health which aims only to diagnose and treat disorders rather than prevent them, had its roots in reforms beginning in the later eighteenth century when the British government was considering care of the insane. Note that this derogatory term denoting mental ill health reflected attitudes of their time. Other terms included 'lunatic', someone considered to have sound memory and understanding but sometimes not, while an 'idiot' was a natural fool from birth.

At this time, those with poor mental health were often cast into houses of correction or, if the family's means allowed, private asylums. There they might be abused, restrained with chains and left to sit in straw soiled with their own faeces. If you were admitted to St Mary of Bethlehem, nicknamed Bedlam, you may have been used for a form of asylum tourism and put on display.

But it was also those instances where people committed to a madhouse were in good mental health that in 1763 inspired the British politician Thomas Townshend to draw together and chair a select committee of the House of Commons to review privately-run madhouses. The inaugural meeting might have gone something like this:

'Confining people in madhouses who are not insane is a shocking state of affairs,' Herbert Mackworth, Member of Parliament, declared to the meeting while pulling his elegant brocade frock coat over his belly squeezing between the buttons of his fashionably tight waistcoat.

'I couldn't agree more,' Townshend replied smoothing the folds of his chins then rubbing his left forefinger over the dimple on the one uppermost. 'We are reliably informed of a number of asylums where proprietors are happy, provided their families pay, to admit people who show signs of neither lunacy nor idiocy.'

Eyebrows elevated around the table accompanied by tutting sounds and shaking of curly, powdered wigs.

'All the same, one would not aim to dispense with madhouses,' answered Mackworth, 'but rather that magistrates were given powers to ensure that inmates received justice.'

Townshend nodded. 'Quite so. Some of these establishments leave their charges in the most appalling conditions. Interposition of legislature, gentlemen, is clearly required,' he concluded with an upward flourish of his left hand.

Townshend's efforts culminated in The Madhouses Act 1774 requiring them to have regular inspections by the Royal College of Physicians. The Lunacy and County Asylum Act 1845 followed, legislation intended to ensure that people suffering from mental ill health were cared for appropriately and with respect. This sounds as enlightened as twenty-first century rehab, although sufferers were not often discharged from county asylums. However, the early twentieth century brought more enlightened attitudes towards psychiatric disorders with the affected often welcomed back to their homes after treatment.

Improvements continued in the 1950s when sedation of patients with psychoses such as bipolar disorder and schizophrenia was replaced with chlorpromazine and lithium carbonate, leading to better targeted psychiatric drugs. At the same time, electroconvulsive therapy, using electricity to induce seizures, although controversial, became recognised as a safe and effective treatment.

So, by the later decades of the twentieth century, we had progressed from the belief that your poor mental ill-health was because you'd made a god angry, to a better knowledge of mental pathologies and recognition of the roles played by life situations, nutritional deficiencies and metabolic disorders. Distinguishing anxiety from anaemia, porphyria from postnatal depression and bipolar disorder from B vitamin deficiency instead of lumping them all together as lunacy, enabled effective treatments. But these approaches did not espouse the doctrine of prevention being better than cure, and overlooked the need for measures which give clinically normal people resilience to life's stresses.

Gerald was a proponent of a resilience-building lifestyle in the 1980s before this was as common as Spotify, the flat white and modernising the monarchy. But I knew others not unlike Gerald.

Alistair Forbes had paint-brush thick, white-grey hair with a forelock that flopped dashingly over his right eye, a determination to run his laboratory with brilliance, and a half-built yacht in his garden.

When the sawing, sanding, splicing and yacht varnishing became onerous, he would turn to his rhubarb patch, which provided the citrusy-smelling offerings with crumbs of earth around the pink, plump roots that he left on colleagues' desks around the time of the summer solstice. 'Kittens and rhubarb are all we give away,' he'd say, winking one sapphire, laser-like iris while shrugging off the thank you's.

Alistair's all-year-round, café-au-lait complexion was acquired through his outdoors-all-weekend habit. And late afternoons on unusually sunny days.

'Get yourselves off home,' he'd say, wandering around the laboratory after his 4p.m. cup of English tea, sipped from a cup and saucer, the prerogative of the head of the lab, while we in the lower orders quaffed Nescafé from mugs. 'It's beautiful out there. Make the most of it.'

Alistair was right, we should have done that. But with worm counts to do and abscesses to culture and blood samples to centrifuge, not to mention the post mortem examination of a dozen dying and desiccated laying fowl, there wasn't the freedom to organise our work as he could do. But he more than made up for it by drinking the late night tea at his desk then being back at work by seven next morning whenever the weather was its dreary English self. He would breeze about the lab in his calf-length white coat, offering his wisdom regardless of whether it was invited, keeping his finger on the pulse and steering us towards his vision of veterinary and scientific excellence.

'What developments, Sheilagh?' he'd demand, drawing his eyebrows like curtains and aiming the sapphire lasers over silver frames, a look that extinguished my cognitive powers, rendering me unable to deliver the update on my work that he wanted.

'Um, well,' I would begin while his eyebrows met in the centre of his head, lowered and with the chin protruding.

'Tell me about the suspected selenium poisoning,' he said, helpfully, on one occasion.

'Oh. Yes. Histology supports that diagnosis and I'm waiting for biochemistry results to confirm.'

Alistair nodded, immobilising me with sapphire. 'You'll write it up, of course.'

'Of course. There'll be more time come the autumn maybe.'

'More time, Sheilagh? What else are your evenings for?'

The simplicity of this rhetoric was Alistair's hallmark. It spoke volumes about what he expected of aspiring pathologists, the sacrifices one should make to publish 'developments' and add a brick to the wall of veterinary knowledge provided, of course, the sun wasn't shining.

But what he showed me was that you can be highly-driven, perfectionist and work long hours yet maintain your mental well-being and boost your psychological resilience with outdoor exercise, offering gifts and by having a hobby, even if the product languished beside abandoned tools gathering weeds, slugs and mouse nests.

When I worked as a new graduate for Henry Taylor, he seemed quite out of love with veterinary practice. He would grumble around the consulting room in his brown twill coat that made him look more like a warehouse gaffer than a vet. Taking the cloth and squeezy bottle from the white stone sink, he'd squirt jeyes on the table then wipe away the dust and hairs from the animal he'd just poked, prodded and pronounced pyrexic, while ash bounced out of the pipe permanently fixed to the corner of his mouth and fell to the floor where he would nudge it with a scuffed brogue.

One afternoon, I assisted him with afternoon surgery. He opened the door to the waiting room.

'Next,' he bellowed across the heads of his clients seated in chairs lined up against the walls.

In struggled old Mr Sansome, a cat basket in each hand. Although it had been only three weeks since I'd taken up post, I'd seen this gentleman twice already, each time with at least four cats.

'Two more outside. Would you mind, dear?' he said to me nodding his head towards the waiting room.

Two orange eyes with large, round, black centres stared out at me from each basket. I lifted them up and took them into the consulting room.

'I'd like you to look at Roger first, please, Mr Taylor,' Mr Sansome said as he released a ball of fur and spit onto the table. 'He's just not himself.'

Henry grumbled and dropped some ash on Roger's head. 'What do you mean?'

'Well, you know, not himself.' The cat lover acquired the look of the cat.

Henry frowned and turned to me. 'Miss Nisbet, take a full history. I need to make a phone call.'

Henry didn't seem pleased to see Mr Sansome. I had a good idea why. The nine cats of Mr Sansome's that I'd examined earlier had been in perfect health but the elderly gentleman would not be convinced of this until he had given their entire life history. Each one reminded him in some specific way of Margaret, his late wife, and although I responded initially with interest, it had begun to wear.

'Is Roger eating as he normally does, Mr Sansome?' I started with the usual questions.

'Goodness, dear, nothing puts Roger off his food. I remember when Margaret and I first collected him from the Cats Protection League in the summer five years ago. No, wait a minute, I tell a lie, it was seven years ago, yes, that's when we got him, must be gone seven years. Yes, seven years … would you believe it. And it was the Dog and Cats Home not the Cats Protection League. I think. Or was it Cats Protection? Anyway, from the start he could eat more than any cat we'd had and he'd even steal food from the dog's bowl,' Mr Sansome chuckled and rubbed the frowning Roger between his flattened ears. 'You're a lad, aren't you, Roger, eh, son?'

A 'yes' would have done, of course.

'Thank you for seeing to Mr Sansome,' Henry said to me later over a cup of coffee, as we sat on the bench beside the autoclave and a bowl of cat testicles awaiting incineration.

I nodded. 'I think the only problem I found in that consultation was poor Mr Sansome's. Why do people bring animals to us with nothing wrong with them?'

Henry removed his pipe from his mouth, crossed his legs and leaned forward, a posture that inevitably heralded a short lecture. 'No one else to talk to. Family far away. Not religious so no priest to help. May not like their neighbours. So they take the pet to the vet. Vets are nice people.'

'But are we the right people to help with chronic loneliness?'

'Sheilagh,' he lowered his voice, reeking with *your youth and inexperience prevent your understanding of my point*, 'we are here to attend. Besides,' he added, replacing the pipe in his mouth and leaning back, 'Mr Sansome pays. Always. In full.'

I wondered at what stage Henry descended from a keen new graduate, as most veterinary graduates are, desperate to advance his skills in the art and science of veterinary medicine, to such disaffection and cynicism. But this notwithstanding, he had remained in general veterinary practice over a period of some thirty years. The key to this perhaps, or one them, was his pastime of topiary, the early Roman art of shaping shrubs into imaginative forms.

'The steady clip-clipping is relaxing,' Henry replied when I asked him during a cat spay what he gained from his hobby, for which he was better known in the town than his people skills.

'But you'd get that with tidying up a hedge wouldn't you?' I asked, tying catgut round an ovary.

Henry nodded while watching me operate. 'Yes, Sheilagh, but when the design that's been in your head for weeks starts to appear, it's so rewarding.'

After I'd located and tied off the other ovary, I glanced up to see Henry's saucers of pupils twinkling like the milky way while he spoke of this diversion from his work.

'So, like pottery, then?' I asked, returning to the cat and finding the cervix.

'Oh no, you're quite wrong there.'

I lifted the uterus and both ovaries through my incision in the cat's flank then looked at Henry.

'My creations, Sheilagh, live and grow.'

I'm not sure Henry was aiming for any sort of godly omnipotence, but what he probably achieved when re-shaping his privet into a series of ducks was flow. Flow was first described by the Hungarian psychologist Mihaly Czikszentmihalyi as the mental state you enter when you're so absorbed in an activity that you lose track of time, and he also noted that creating something was more important than completing it. So Alistair was right in not rushing to float his boat.

Wellness is another recent concept that recognises, amongst other things, that the state of our mental health can influence our physical health and vice versa. So, chronic physical pain can cause us emotional distress which in turn amplifies our pain, possibly leaving us fatigued, anxious and angry.

When I spent one summer with redoubtable veterinary surgeon, Gordon Macrae, I wasn't long out of a blazer and gymslip and had enjoyed such good health that I couldn't appreciate the effect of chronic pain on mood. The only time during my extramural placement with Gordon that I saw the pink and fluffy side of his nature was when he addressed his Cairn terriers.

'Deoch, Doris, come on now, ye wee toe-rags, into the car,' he called to them one day as we prepared for a farm visit.

They jumped in and turned round and round in circles in the seat behind me, filling the car with a blast of terrier, then curling up on their rumpled tartan rug.

'Right, off we go. We've a herd TB and Brucella test to do,' Gordon stated as he eased himself, inch-by-inch, into the driving seat then started the engine.

Two fawn muzzles soon appeared between the blue vinyl front seats and nudged Gordon's left elbow.

'Och, come on then, ye wee tikes.'

This was Gordon's signal for Deoch and Doris to wriggle round and settle on his thighs. They were small enough to fit in the space between the bottom of the steering wheel and Gordon's lanky legs, looking as if it were made for them. The whole picture was as incongruous as a bar and pool table in St Giles Cathedral and I had to focus my mind on bovine tuberculosis and brucellosis to prevent overt mirth.

I glanced at Gordon's profile with its high-bridged nose like a Shire horse supported by a beech hedge of a moustache. All his visible clothes, down to the bow-tie, were checked tweed and his fat-depleted shoulders formed wee bumps in the top of his jacket. The flaky surfaces of his ears held a flat tweed cap that I rarely saw him remove and I imagined him wearing it sitting up in bed in checked tweed pyjamas and his round spectacles to read veterinary journals.

'There was an article in the Veterinary Record about the growing number of vet students who have antibodies to brucellosis,' I said as we left the outskirts of the town.

Gordon gave a slow up and down movement of the head that indicated he was preparing a careful argument.

'All vets in large animal practice have brucellosis to some extent. I've certainly got my fair share but I'm lucky I'm not too badly affected. I know a few others who suffer with such severe fevers and joint pains they can't practice any more.'

'How do they get it?'

'Attending a calving cow with the disease, mostly.'

It was time for Deoch and Doris to swap places. They seemed to have an agreement to do this after about twenty minutes of travel so they each got a chance of looking out the driver's window.

Gordon glanced down with an avuncular smile. 'Steady, ye wee tikes,' he murmured.

'So we're testing for both TB and Brucella today?' I asked.

Gordon nodded then cleared his throat, lifted his chin and flared his nostrils, behaviours I'd come to recognise as the harbinger of a series of questions that would make the Nuremberg Trials seem like a pub quiz.

'We inject each cow on the first day of the test with two types of PPD,' he glanced at me over the Shire horse nose. I nodded. He went on. 'What are they?'

'One is avian, the other bovine.'

'What?'

Some of his questions were cryptic and required a clear memory of his introductory statements. I hesitated then continued. 'PPD.'

'And what is that?' Gordon persisted, his voice raised enough to cause Deoch and Doris to give a simultaneous upward glance.

'Oh, yes, sorry.' I'd lost count of the number of times I'd said sorry to Gordon. 'Purified protein derivative.'

After we'd arrived at the farm, Gordon frowned and

closed his eyes as he pulled himself out of the car. His back creaked as he bent down to untie his laces, take off his shoes and pull on wellingtons.

We collected the equipment we needed from the boot of the car then joined Sam, the herdsman, next to the cattle crush in the cow shed. Gordon donned a leather belt with a holster on each side of his waist, then stood like a cowboy minus the jaunty neck scarf and scorpion-picking pointed-toe boots.

He loaded the TB syringes with PPD, put one in each holster, then brought out a notebook and pen from the pocket of his brown coat.

'Take these,' he said to me. 'Note the ear numbers and the skin thickness readings when I give you them.'

Gordon turned to Sam. 'Didn't see your wife at the choral group last night.'

Sam shook his head and brought a cow into the cattle crush. 'No, Aileen's away seeing her sister. She'll be back next week, though. Enjoys it, so she does.'

Gordon nodded. 'Aye, it's good for the body and the soul is singing,' he said as he grasped the ear tag of the cow in the crush. '03503, Sheilagh. Do you sing?' he asked as he measured the thickness of the cow's skin.

I scribbled the ear number in the notebook. 'Not since school,' I answered. 'I was press-ganged into taking part in Vivaldi's Gloria.'

'Ah, a fine piece of music. Avian seven, bovine nine. Why did you stop going to choir?'

I put a seven in the column marked A and a nine in the one marked B. 'Well, it was a bit boring, I suppose.'

Gordon injected the cow's skin with both PPDs, then with a wrinkle of his beech hedge, turned to me.

'Boring, Sheilagh? Boring? Singing is as good for you as a brisk walk. Blood tube.'

I handed him the tube with needle.

'Aileen says it tones up her tummy muscles, too,' Sam added, with a smile and a wink, restoring some levity to proceedings.

Gordon nodded, straight-faced. 'Yes indeed. All round beneficial activity. Next cow, Sam.'

I found it hard work seeing practice with Gordon. But there was no doubt that brucellosis played havoc with his joints and, I appreciate now, probably explained his temper as short as a Cairn terrier's legs. But, long before the concepts of flow and wellness, Gordon embraced coping strategies. His interest in all things choral as well as his warming relationship with Deoch and Doris no doubt increased his resilience to physical pain, while accepting his illness and knowing that he was not alone in suffering brucellosis probably helped him gain control over it.

Coping strategies are elements of mindful living, which is now widely accepted as benefiting mental and physical well-being. Mindfulness and meditation no longer go hand-in-hand with a rainbow of prayer flags, a number one haircut and strappy sandals. It's even okay to admit to starting your day with a salute to the sun and a cup of milk-thistle tea accompanied by haunting melodies of the Indian flute.

Practices that increase personal resilience are included in the Mind Matters Initiative launched by the

Royal College of Veterinary Surgeons in 2014. This, and Vetlife, a charity that provides a 24/7 helpline, arose from the growing concern about poor mental health in the veterinary profession in which stress, depression, anxiety and suicidal thoughts are, unfortunately, not rare.

It would be difficult to address some of the factors responsible for this, for example our propensity for perfectionism and access to drugs allowing a quick suicide. But stress can be reduced in veterinary workplaces with training, for example, in how to deal with exposure to animal suffering and client bereavement. Support from colleagues and ensuring there are sufficient members of staff for the workload are other interventions.

Not an issue of some veterinary publications goes by without an article on mental well-being. Healthy lifestyle programmes and culture change to reduce stigma and encourage help-seeking behaviour are part of mental health awareness training now provided to the veterinary profession.

But in times when psychological disturbance was synonymous with weak-mindedness, lacking in self-discipline and lurching towards the loopy, and when we talked about maintaining high standards of welfare and well-being we meant that of animals, not the vets taking care of them, Gordon, Henry, Gerald and Alistair were my priceless mentors. They showed me the importance of acquiring new skills, physical exercise, acts of kindness and close relationships with others, including Cairn terriers, when our lives become stressful or we suffer chronic pain or when our jobs no longer inspire us. And indeed, I have found these measures anodynes in some challenging times.

A number of my colleagues have not been as fortunate. Our profession is a small one and, tragically, many of us know someone who has taken their own life. Good mental health amongst vets can be as elusive as tender loving care in an eighteenth century madhouse and, although we aren't at the stage yet where anxiety and depression are as disclosable as angina and dyspepsia, the RCVS initiatives along with more supportive and informed societal attitudes to mental ill-health are much welcomed.

7

TERMS AND CONDITIONS

The veterinary lexicon is like clootie dumpling: old-fangled, obscure, rich, heterogeneous and a bit of a mouthful. To help with this, sometimes the name of the person who first described a condition is used rather than the condition itself. I expect you'd find Key-Gaskell syndrome more digestible than feline dysautonomia, and pronouncing Addison's disease instead of hypoadrenocorticism causes loss of neither saliva nor dignity.

Regional variations of various disease names exist, too. For example, it was only after several months in my first job in practice I realised that the diseases referred to by the large animal medicine department at Glasgow as chooberkullosus and burroosullosus were identical to the occasional suspect cases of bovine TB and brucella infection I met in Lincolnshire. In the same county, by the way, I came to know that Toozday follows Monday, a buhh chuh is a purveyor of animal products and an acceptable response to 'eh up me duck' is fine, thank you, how are you.

I came to know other non-veterinary yet essential terms when I worked in East Yorkshire. A foe kinn obb edd, for example, is a rather silly person, bliddynew sins refers to an impediment to normal progress and one might enjoy a meal with pittay tuz and a coe pahtae to wash them down.

Vets are amongst many groups of people who use acronyms. These save time, they're easier to say than the full versions and they make us sound less pedantic when having discussions amongst colleagues. You may have seen an acronym or two on the records your vet keeps for your pet. For example NAD means nothing abnormal detected and DUDE stands for defaecating, urinating, drinking and eating. And on account of the plethora of police dramas on television you will probably understand a warning along the lines of 'going AWOL in your car if you have an ASBO due to ABH may result in you being ANPR'd and chased by an ARV'.

However, the compulsion to speak in acronyms all the time carries the danger of sounding pompous. I had one enigmatic senior colleague whose fulminating acronymitis was manifested as sentences consisting of entire strings of the things and enough to make a scene from the BBC's *Line of Duty* relatively understandable. I had just started working in his team when he mystified me by describing the work of UKASTA and the iterative actions of the FAO and WHO and how this had enormous implications for ADAS and the CAP. I won't bore you with the meanings of these and, on reflection, maybe that's why my senior colleague used them when speaking to me.

Urban dictionaries are full of acronyms describing a plethora of social anxieties, like the FOMO you might have if you've been invited to an event, don't want to go but go anyway due to your fear of missing out. It's only when you reach an age of philosophical reflection that you experience JOMO by declining such invitations and enjoy the joy of missing out. There's also YOLO which those of my generation don't feel it too onerous to replace with you only live once, and a host of others that can summed up less abstrusely as varying forms of cognition.

Our medical colleagues have an array of colourful and expressive acronyms. Tf bundy, meaning 'totally f***ed but unfortunately not dead yet' might be used when doctors are faced with terminal cases that to describe fully to each other would be unpleasant and stressful. Instead, in four syllables, they can summarise the state-of-play with a patient and their grave prognosis, although I feel sure they would select other words to communicate with the patient's family.

Occasional animal tf bundys have been presented to me. One such was a cow that I arrived to find lying on her side, neck stretched out, panting and muscles twitching. Tim, the farmer was standing beside me but otherwise doing much the same things. He lifted his greasy cap, rubbed his hairless pate with it, and replaced it before bending down with the creaking sound of a sapling in high winds and placing a dinner-plate sized hand on each of his knees.

'Wha' d'ya reckon?' he asked as I knelt beside the poor beast and got out my stethoscope.

The grass warming my legs and the buttercups scattered through the pasture like sprinkles on a cupcake seemed at odds with this apparently terminal and tf bundy case.

I didn't say as much to Tim, a practising Methodist and stalwart of the village carpet bowls federation, and certainly not about one of his herd that he seemed to value as much as the distaff side of his family – a formidable wife, president of the Women's Institute, and four teenage daughters. He appeared less scared of his cattle, though.

'Hmm,' I said as I removed the ear pieces of the stethoscope, 'when did she calve, Tim?'

'Aye, it'll be fow-er days gone. Not been right since.'

This confirmed my thoughts that her problems had begun with one of the post-calving disorders caused by an imbalance in the minerals calcium, magnesium and phosphorous, but had then progressed to muscle damage and other problems. Downer-cows, we call them, and a lot of them 'go down the road', the euphemism for calling in the knacker man.

Tim and I agreed the likely prognosis, but he asked me to do what I could. I knew the cow wouldn't be used for human consumption, so there was nothing to lose in treating her with a bit of everything – minerals, steroids, a vitamin concoction that made your hands smell of Marmite, and probably a shot of some antibiotic although this would be frowned upon now.

'Expect you'll be giving Paddy a call soon. I'm sorry

Tim,' I said as I got up and replaced bottles and tubes in my treatment box.

Tim agreed that the knacker's journey would probably not be wasted.

After I'd got back to the practice, the receptionist called to me as I was in the yard cleaning and replenishing the boot of my car, serenaded by Steve Wright on the car radio.

'Paddy's on the phone for you, Sheilagh.'

'What does he want?' I called back.

'Needs a word.'

I abandoned my boot ablutions and walked up the corridor to the office.

'That cow you saw at Somerton?' Paddy began cryptically.

'Uh huh?'

'Well, Tim said to come for her, like, then half an hour later he rings and says don't. She's okay. Running round the field, like.'

'That's good news, Paddy. Didn't expect that.'

'No, me neither. D'you think there's something funny going on?'

'How d'you mean?'

'Well, you know, thinking she can go for slaughter at the abattoir instead, like.'

'Shouldn't think so. I'll ring Tim and get the story.'

I didn't have to ring Tim – he called almost as soon as I'd ended the call with Paddy.

'Dunno which of your treatments did the trick, Sheilagh, but that cow got up minutes after you'd gone. Grazing with the others as if nothing had happened to her.'

I'd no idea what the secret had been either, but the moral of this story was, not all tf bundys may be quite so totally f***ed.

TTR, 'tooth tattoo ratio', is another wonderful acronym originating in human medicine but applicable to veterinary work. It may seem unkind but, as a general rule, I found that clients with few teeth and a large number of tattoos, and therefore a low TTR, needed more help in complying with my instructions regarding the care of their pets. Inferences over their likelihood of paying the fee might also be drawn from the TTR.

'Ma dug's nae weel,' the man with a voice like metal over gravel wheezed down the line to me one Saturday evening when I was on call.

'I'm sorry to hear that. Can you tell me a bit more about your dog, please?' I asked.

'Ach, she's spewin' a'where an' awfa' thirsty, ken,' the wheeze continued.

'Better bring her along to the practice,' I replied.

I waited alone for the man to arrive with his nae weel dug, then invited them into a consulting room. 'Troy' introduced himself and his dog, 'Tess'.

'Please lift Tess onto the table,' I asked Troy.

Then I looked at the lowest TTR I had ever seen.

Troy's mouth was devoid of incisors and one lonely upper canine stood stalactite-like at the corner of his mouth. What visible flesh was not tattooed in an array of colour that would shame any rainbow, was spray-tanned and filled with metal. There was a whiff of something that may have been something of the Class B group and his abdomen would have made a healthy full term triplet pregnancy. His head was shaved along the sides and an intricate Celtic design in dark blue and green adorned the hairless areas. A lilac vest, that may once have been white, and jeans that seemed strangers to a washing machine were his only clothes. The menacing look was completed with big, black lace up boots. I controlled my palpitations by concentrating on the dog.

Tess, a Staffordshire Bull Terrier, looked very depressed and I soon saw the tell-tale pus from her vulva that suggested pyometra – a condition where the womb fills with pus and makes the dog very ill.

'She'll need an operation to remove her womb,' I advised Mr Low TTR. 'We'll need to do this as soon as she is fit for surgery, so you'll have to leave her with us, I'm afraid.'

Troy looked at me, squeezing his eyebrows together, then gave a gasp which exposed the stalactite.

'Wull she be a' reet, though? I dae ma best fur 'er, ye ken. Un aw-purr-ae-shun? Um awfa' worrit.'

'We'll do our best for her, too, of course, and let you know how she is after her op,' I replied.

Tess's womb was almost as big as the rest of her, but she coped with surgery well and was able to be discharged a few days later. When she saw Troy, she bounded up to him and leaped into his arms, then began licking the tears that ran down his face.

'Thank ye, thank ye sae much,' he said between sobs and licks.

I was misty-eyed myself with this reunion. 'Keep an eye on the wound in her tummy and bring her back for us to check her over in a week,' I said.

He nodded. 'Canna pay ye now, please?'

This question took me aback, but I recovered and led Troy, still in a warm embrace with Tess, to reception where his invoice was soon prepared. With the emergency call out and operation it ran into the sort of figure that makes you inhale uncontrollably as if you'd plunged naked into icy water, and a client with a high TTR may well have requested to pay in instalments.

But when Troy saw his bill, he nodded and gestured to his back pocket. I pulled out a wad of notes then counted out what was needed.

'An' tak anither,' he said to me, nodding his colourful scalp, 'fur yer trouble.'

I thanked him, asked the receptionist to put the note in the tea fund, and resolved never again to judge a low TTR's looks by their colours.

Another practice where I worked had a plethora of large, airy, empty and unused operating theatres; a portent of business parks built on early twenty-first century sub-prime hope then abandoned with the economic collapse a few years later. But this practice had built up a large client-base, too, and ran busy surgeries lasting several hours each creating long operating lists that we tackled in the one theatre in use. The nurses embraced the concepts of recycling to the extent of washing needles and syringes after each use then sterilising them in the 'Little Sister' autoclave, but overall it was a happy team, notwithstanding the workload.

Every practice has a particular range of drugs and I soon got used to those that the boss selected. But one drug

I couldn't fathom was a bubble-gum coloured liquid that the nurses dispensed from a flagon into small bottles then labelled them 'PEL'.

Poly ethyl something, maybe. Pro emesis liquid? Nah. Pre enteric lubricant? I gave up.

'What does that mean?' I asked Naimh, one of the nurses, as I pointed to the label.

She looked in the direction of my finger. 'What?' she asked.

'That,' I replied.

Naimh looked at me and frowned. 'PEL you mean?'

I nodded.

'Pink ear lotion,' she said, still frowning and shaking her head.

Another acronym first came to my attention on my first night on call in a busy city practice. It had gone midnight when the nurse who had drawn the short straw of being on call with me, rang to tell me about a client who was on her way to the practice with her chihuahua, Hamlet, who had just been hit by a car.

'Better come quick, Sheilagh,' Fiona said, 'or he'll be PU.'

'Peayou?'

'Paws up. You know, er, dead. Doesn't sound hopeful. Mrs Graham thinks he's lost a lot of blood.'

I pulled on jeans and a sweat shirt over my pyjamas, kissed my greyhound, Jasper, goodbye, promising him I'd be back soon then leapt into my car. I had got half way to the practice when I saw a flashing blue light in the rear view mirror. I cursed at having to waste the time it took to pull over to let him pass then realised with a plunging of my stomach to my feet, that the pulling in of the police car in front of me suggested it was me they wanted to speak to.

'Yes, officer?' I asked with as much courtesy as I could muster in view of my urgent need to get to the practice.

'Are you aware you are driving with your head lights off?' he asked, rather rhetorically, I thought.

Of course I wasn't aware I'd forgotten to put my lights on else they'd be on, I felt like saying but decided a simple no, sorry, would be more likely to bring this incident to an end.

'Where are you going?' he asked.

I explained the purpose of my journey and its haste. He thought for what seemed like a minute then concluded that he would let me continue but would follow me to my destination.

The policeman decided he'd better come into the practice, too in order to verify my account of a dog requiring urgent attention. Fiona met us as she left the consulting room and raised her eyebrows when she saw my escort.

'How is the dog?' I asked.

'He's not pea ... I mean he is quite poorly,' Fiona answered.

Evidently speechless with concern, the officer followed me into the consulting room, but my irritation with him evaporated when it became clear that offsetting Mrs Graham's worries was her inference that I'd secured a police escort to hasten my journey to attend to Hamlet.

'Thank you for going to all this trouble to see us,' she said, nodding to the officer.

'Nothing at all, Mrs Graham,' I assured her. 'We'll take Hamlet through to theatre and look at him more closely there.'

Happily, Hamlet's injuries were treatable and his paws remained firmly down. And as a bonus the officer was content with my story and advised that he would be taking my driving peccadillo no further.

But I came across the epitome of acronym use when I was a house surgeon with the privilege of learning from some renowned small animal surgeons. They worked hard and enjoyed a varied caseload referred to them by colleagues in general practice and assisting them gave me invaluable surgical experience.

But my surgical idols played hard, too. Doing a 'poets' (p*ss off early tomorrow's Saturday) was an established Friday afternoon activity, while they would go to the Foreign Office (f**k off) only in particularly troublesome times.

I came across their most used acronym when I had the undoubted honour of meeting Miss Phemie Macpherson-Muir. The embodiment of comfortable, middle-aged, middle-class chic, she had woolly-stockinged into one of the consulting rooms one morning cuddling Ernst, her miniature Dachshund, wrapped in cashmere tartan. A stratus of lavender floated above her taupe felt hat sitting at a jaunty angle and adorned with three magnificent pheasant feathers. Between the hat and her lightly-rouged temples cumulus clumps of hair made bids for freedom and her large ear lobes each clutched a gold-set, yet understated, pearl. She bore her facial lines with evident pride, each testament to a life most likely lived in Presbyterian moderation.

She flared the nostrils of her aquiline nose as she addressed me. 'Ay-ve brought Ernst. For Mr Sand's attention,' she inclined her head slightly to the side to stress that Ernst was to be put in hands no less prestigious than the most senior orthopaedic surgeon.

'Yes, of course, Miss Macpherson-Muir,' I said and held out my arms to take the cashmere-cocooned treasure. 'Please ring us this afternoon for a report on Ernst's progress.'

She re-did the top button in her well-worn yet tidy tweed coat, nodded and left while I carried my precious cargo to the kennels for his pre-surgery checks.

'Surgery department,' I said later that day after I'd picked up the phone for Janet, the surgical secretary, who was busy putting letters into envelopes and addressing them with white sticky labels. The house surgeon was also at times the house skivvy. 'Can I help you?'

'Hair-low. Ay-am phayning about may dawg.'

I recognised Phemie Macpherson-Muir's euphonious tones with that affected posh accent where the 'ah' sound is pronounced 'ay' so that a creche is a collision amongst vehicles and sex is a means of packaging coal and potatoes.

'Certainly, Miss Macpherson-Muir,' I replied, 'I'll make enquiries about Ernst for you now. Please hold.'

I left the office and walked into the corridor where there was a large white-board on which updates for all surgical cases were posted. There were four columns: name of animal; surgeon's name; procedure carried out; state-of-play. The fourth column for Ernst was blank. My heart gave a leap.

'Livvy,' I said to the senior nurse who was wiping down stainless steel surfaces at the same time as packing washed surgical equipment for sterilisation and while moving dog bowls into a corner with her foot. 'What's happened to Miss Macpherson-Muir's dog?'

'Which dog?'

'Ernst. The mini Daschsy.'

'Oh, yes. Had his op. Went well. He's comfortable and ay-wack-bay,' she replied while she enrobed a theatre pack with tape and tore it with her teeth. 'Haven't had time to put it on the board, yet. Sorry.'

'And he's awa-what?' I asked.

She stopped and looked towards me. 'A.W.A.C.B.E.,' she spelled out. 'As well as can be expected.'

I continued to use this acronym throughout my career and even now, I find it can be applied to many situations. So, after a mediocre holiday, or a hard day at work I may be awacbe and I recall long sleepless nights with my newborn children where the following day I would be perfectly described as awacbe. Andy Murray's play was awacbe soon after his hip surgery. And I suppose we could say the same about the performance of the beleaguered Theresa May regarding Brexit negotiations.

We vets have come up with a few useful phrases, too, and one perfect example was the inspiration of a dear colleague, Fred, our post-mortem room attendant,

'Six chickens, a calf, three lambs and a badger,' Fred called through the hatch between the post-mortem room and laboratory when I asked what had arrived for examination.

I was on post-mortem duty. This meant that I considered samples that came in through the post and decided what tests we needed to do on them, carried out necropsies on entire animals submitted to us and took telephone calls from vets in practice who needed our help with various disease problems on their clients' farms. In one lab where I worked, one of the passengers taking an afternoon bus into town was a leak-proof box of well-wrapped samples – blood, urine, poo, maybe bits of dead sheep – sent for our attention by a veterinary practice.

I liked pathology. It helped me use a lot of the information I had seared into my neurons by burning every last molecule of undergraduate midnight oil. General practice was interesting, but a lot of the same things made me wonder why I'd worked so hard to amass so much detail about so many diseases.

I started on the calf because it was the biggest animal and after my post-mortem examination Fred could be cutting it up into oven ready chunks and incinerating it while I got on with the chickens and lambs. It was well-thought out. The work flowed.

'Made a rhubarb crumble with vanilla custard last night,' I told Fred as I cut into a pathologically-perfect abscess on the surface of the calf's liver. Yellow, curdled pus oozed out and onto the putrefied redness of the liver beneath. 'Let's get some of that,' I said to Fred and pointed to the abscess.

Fred nodded, brought a plastic bottle and scooped up some pus.

'Sounds nice,' he replied. 'Haven't had crumble since I started this diet malarkey. All low cal, low fat, low taste, low fun, low everything.'

We worked on like a well-maintained engine.

'Where'd you put the badger?' I asked Fred once everything else had been examined, sampled and incinerated.

Fred smiled. 'Think you might struggle with it.'

In the 1980s, road-killed badgers were brought to us to screen for bovine TB. This meant we looked for typical post mortem signs and took samples of various glands to culture for the bacteria that cause this disease. Some of the badgers were freshly dead, and we could give them, and most of the others, a thorough examination. Those that had been lying around in several days of summer heat were like barrage balloons with four little limbs attached. They gave a soft pop when you inserted a knife into them and the glands we needed along with everything else inside had become one communal liquid. But the most difficult to necropsy were the badgers that had been lying on the motorway for any length of time.

I looked on the post mortem table at the two dimensional piece of black and white hair that would have made a decorative floor covering near one's bedside.

'Ah. See what you mean, Fred. Another carpet badger,'

I shrugged my shoulders and started rooting around for the pancaked glands we needed.

Another lovely phrase was that inspired by manual pregnancy diagnosis in cattle. This is an art acquired through long years of practice at what initially feels like that blindfolded party game where you have to guess by palpation the identities of various objects placed before you.

As undergraduates in Glasgow, we were introduced to pregnancy diagnosis with weekly visits to the herd at the Cochno estate where the poor animals were tethered in individual stalls by the neck, leaving their hind quarters vulnerable to the inchoate arms of vet students. I think most of the cows were used to it and they munched their hay contentedly while we guddled around in their rectums trying to feel for their ovaries and wombs. The cow's reproductive tract lies just underneath her rectum, so by putting your arm inside the latter right up to your shoulder you can feel the ovaries and uterus through the wall of the rectum. Even though we wore arm-length gloves, we always returned from Cochno visits oozing bucolic aromas. These offended the delicate sensibilities of my medic flat-mates to the point that they had a kettle of boiling water waiting for myself and Liz, the other vet student in the flat, so that we could wash thoroughly before the whole airspace was indistinguishable from a slurry tank.

Experienced colleagues can detect very early pregnancies, and also distinguish growing follicles in the ovaries from ruptured ones, but even they are sometimes challenged by what they find.

'What's the earliest pregnancy you've correctly diagnosed?' I asked Richard on one of his visits to our lab which inevitably started in the tea room with a good laugh and giggle about his playing the organ for his local church. With a knowledge of only three chords he claimed he could accompany the entire New English Hymnal.

Richard, who worked for a company concerned with bovine genetics and reproduction, did a lot of manual pregnancy diagnosis in cattle, although he seemed to avoid smelling like it.

'Ooo. Now then. Probably about five to six weeks. Varies of course. Heifers are more difficult, I find. I've got a few cows to do at Fosters where we're visiting together to look into their infertility problem, so you can have a go, if you like.'

'That's kind, Richard,' I said, 'but I'll be concentrating on getting a sheath washing from a bull. Happy to watch you while I do this, though.'

We were looking for an organism called Campylobacter, which can cause abortion or make it difficult to get cows into calf, and a bull can carry the organism in his sheath. So, after sedating the bull on this farm, and he was lying down, I poured a sterile solution into his sheath then gave it a good, all over massage before collecting the solution into a bottle for later culture.

I looked up when I'd finished. 'How's it going, Richard?'

'Six weeks that one,' he answered. 'Would that fit with your records, Bill?' he asked Mr Foster who seemed unable to take his eyes off the clip board in front of him while I was busy with his bull.

'Aye, about right. Six weeks ago she was served, right enough.'

Richard's arm went into cow after cow and he seemed to be doing rather well.

The last cow was put in the stall, ready for Richard.

'This one's a bit funny, Richard,' Bill said. 'I think the Hereford served her, but she wasn't bulling for very long.'

It wasn't surprising, given the problem on the farm, that one cow would be difficult to get in calf, but Richard examined her anyway. He was ages with his arm in her rectum, then he tried the other arm, then back to the first, a look of determined bewilderment on his face.

'What do you think, Richard?' I asked. 'Any sign that she's in calf?'

Richard took his arm out of the cow and shrugged. 'Too dark to tell,' he said.

Amongst us all, we got the Campylobacter infection under control and the cows that had been 'too dark to tell' later gave enlightened and convincing six week pregnancies.

No review of veterinary words and phrases would be complete without mention of the mnemonics, without which I may not have survived the gruelling anatomy lessons of my undergraduate days. One is 'toilet paper my ass' which stands for the valves of the heart: triscuspid, pulmonary, mitral, aortic. The mnemonic for the direction of blood flow is a little cleaner: 'plenty of very attractive beauties visit cellulite (removal) places and lie' which acts as a reminder for pulmonary vein – aorta – body – vena cava – pulmonary artery – lungs.

But proving the rule for mnemonics that the more obscene they are, the more memorable they become is one for the twelve cranial nerves. It is so unprintable I dare not even hint it and now, forty odd years on, my memory cells still clutch it with the tenacity of a kitchen to burnt toast. But it allows me to recite with ease the olfactory, optic, oculomotor, trochlear, trigeminal, abducens, facial, vestibulocochlear, glossopharyngeal, vagus, spinal accessory and hypoglossal nerves.

Now you see what I mean about clootie dumpling.

8

WE SHOOT HORSES

'Do what for the local authority?' I asked my boss in a veterinary practice where I worked as he tidied the drugs and equipment in the boot of his car.

'Stray dog control, Sheilagh. Put down the ones their kennel staff bring to you. Leave the bodies – they'll see to that – but note the numbers.'

'How many will there be?'

'Varies. A dozen maybe. Take one of the nurses to help. Make sure you've got plenty pentobarb.'

'Euthanase a dozen dogs?'

The boss nodded while wiping bottles of penicillin and tetracycline then juxtaposing them in a box. 'Won't take you long. The staff there know the drill.'

'But I've never done that to so many dogs at once.'

The boss stopped what he was doing and turned to look at me. 'Sheilagh,' he said without one atom of compromise, 'this has to be done, so please do so.' He returned to tidying his boot. 'The kennels are on your way back from afternoon surgery at Haynes Road.'

Dreading this task, I took Jane, a veterinary nurse with several more years of practice experience than I had. She gave me directions along a track, got out of the car to open a steel gate with barbed-wire topped fencing on either side then we drove on towards a red brick building. Its windows were opaque with years of dirt and cobwebs. I parked, took my black medicines bag containing needles, syringes, pentobarbitone and a stethoscope and we walked towards the building. Ragwort lined the path where haggard weeds poked between the cobbles and as we approached a door that was well past its salad days, I could see piles of cigarette butts at one side. I knocked.

A woman with short, grey-streaked brown hair opened the door. Smoking, stress, age or all three had left her face furrowed with wrinkles.

'Hi, Jane. Is this your new vet?' she asked nodding towards my bag then looking at me with a smile that wasn't reflected in her eyes. Her teeth like weathered gravestones confirmed her exposure to tobacco. 'I'm Babs, kennel superintendent. Come in.'

I introduced myself then we followed Babs down a corridor that wouldn't have been out of place in Colditz. Electrical wires struggled out between polystyrene roof tiles and grasped light bulbs shaded only by dust. I shivered and inhaled the mixing odours of bleach and dog excrement.

Babs opened a door at the end of the corridor and led us into a stone-floored room with kennels along both sides. The dogs in the first few kennels eye-balled us and barked. Puppies, old animals and all ages in-between stood on their hind legs, front paws on the kennel fronts.

'These ones haven't been here long,' Babs said, 'we won't be bringing them out today.'

Bringing them out today. As good a euphemism as stray dog control.

'Penny,' she called to a thin, aetiolated girl standing outside the kennels at the end of the room, 'get collars and leads on the ones in kennels R to V then ask Kate to help you bring them in next door, two at a time.'

'How long have these dogs been here?' I asked, nodding to those I was about to meet.

'At least a week,' Babs replied. 'Depends on the numbers coming in and how many we find homes for.'

She led us into a remorseless room, concrete walls and floor, central drain and a single light bulb hanging from the ceiling.

Penny and Kate brought the dogs to us in ark-like consignments. Jane held the first dog and I lifted his left foreleg and felt for a vein. I could not hold his look – two brown eyes endowing me with a trust that in seconds I would prove undeserving. I made the lethal injection. He lost consciousness right away. I took the stethoscope and listened for an absent heart beat, saw his chest fall for the last time and felt the stare of his eyes as they became marbles in his warm head.

We went through them leaving corpse after corpse behind us; a length of the unwanted and now lifeless; a man-made solution to a man-made problem.

Afterwards, we walked back up the corridor and into a small cloakroom where we washed our hands in a filthy sink. No one said anything.

Once we were outside, Babs put a hand in the pocket of her navy body-warmer, pulled out a packet of cigarettes, took one out and as she placed it in her mouth I saw that her finger nails were bitten to the quick. From the other pocket she took out a lighter and held it to the cigarette, sucking air through it.

'I'm not sure who'll be coming next time, Babs,' I said as I opened the boot of my car and placed my bag inside.

She shrugged. 'That's fine. I'll be here anyway.'

'Are you always around for this?' I asked.

She drew on her cigarette, long and deep, holding her breath before exhaling grey smoke through her nostrils then mouth.

'Uh-huh. I like to make sure it goes okay, you know?'

I nodded and got in the car, tears clawing their way out of my eyes. Jane sat in the passenger seat, ran her hands through her short blonde hair and looked out the windscreen. Both of us were mute.

We were a mile from the practice when I broke the silence. 'I forgot to count them.'

'Sixteen,' Jane replied.

'Sixteen,' I whispered.

I drove into the practice car park, pulled up and switched off the engine. 'Jane, does this get any easier?' I asked before she got out.

She looked at me, then said, 'You wouldn't want it to.'

I know humane destruction helps manage unwanted

pet animals. It can be the path of least suffering for them. I know that. I know. It reduces the population of feral animals, breeding uncontrolled. Their alternative is neglect, starvation, abuse or kennelling with little human contact. I know all that. But these arguments did nothing to temper my utter despair that February afternoon when I questioned why my long years of training to treat animals had ended in killing them in such quantity.

Euthanasing any animal is unpleasant.

But when vets are admitted to the Royal College of Veterinary Surgeons they make a declaration which includes the words, '… my constant endeavour will be to ensure the health and welfare of animals committed to my care.' This, with the animal welfare legislation and the RCVS Code of Conduct for Veterinary Surgeons, provides vets with the privilege of relieving an animal's suffering by putting it to sleep. They do this in specific circumstances, when both they and the animal's keeper feel sure there is no action that better serves the animal's welfare.

In contrast, the Suicide Act 1961 and the General Medical Council's Good Medical Practice guidelines prevent doctors in the United Kingdom from assisting patients to die. Additionally, some doctors on graduating take variations of the Hippocratic Oath, which may include an undertaking not to prescribe a lethal drug nor give advice that may cause death.

These ethical and legislative constraints on doctors condemn their patients diagnosed with a painful and terminal disease to dying at some point in pain and distress. You may find it equally unappealing to end your life in a prolonged period of the total dementia described by Shakespeare as, 'in second childishness and mere oblivion, sans teeth, sans eyes, sans taste, sans everything.'

I have a colleague whose wife had liver cancer. A variety of treatments had failed to stem her aggressive disease and he was obliged to watch her die in extreme pain.

'She begged me to end her suffering,' he said, 'as I wouldn't have hesitated to do had she been one of my patients. But we both knew I couldn't do that for her.'

My Dachshund, Barty, was only eight years old when a prolapsed disc caused such damage to his spinal cord that he became paralysed and incontinent. I knew there was only one reasonable course of action, but I nursed him for a day or two before coming to terms with putting him to sleep. Lucky was our grey Connemara pony who had helped numerous children to ride including my son Hamish. Lucky knew all the mounted pony games. Weaving in and out of bollards? Easy. Putting flags in cones? Bring it on. And although the egg and spoon race was his forte, whatever new game was played, Lucky played it like he'd played it all his life, got the rosette then was back in his stable munching hay, heedless to his success. We don't know how old he was – his passport issued in 2004 said 'at least seventeen' – but in 2010 he developed a serious disease, malignant melanoma, lost weight on ample spring grass, had no interest in riding out and looked quite unlike his name.

So, as autumn approached, I called in the huntsman. Of course it was hard saying goodbye to a pony who had done so much for so many children; of course I wept when I heard the pistol fire; and of course, as for Barty, euthanasia was better for Lucky than the slow, lingering and painful death he would have likely suffered had he been human.

Human euthanasia, where doctors administer a lethal drug to relieve suffering, and assisted dying, helping someone to end their life, are currently permitted in a number of European countries, parts of America, Japan and South Korea. All of these countries currently deny such services to foreigners except Switzerland.

So, if you are terminally ill in the United Kingdom and wish to choose when to end your life, you may commit suicide, which is not against the law, or you may go to Switzerland for an assisted death. Neither option is for the faint-hearted, and while they both take courage and determination, the latter option requires, amongst other things, a lot of money, sufficient mobility to travel, and a willingness to end your life in a foreign country away from your home and loved ones.

So, current UK law respects human life and tries to avoid the potential for someone being forced to have an assisted death, but it doesn't help you if you are dying in agony.

If you have a terminal illness, your doctor will probably be unwilling to talk to you about assisted dying, but if you have an elderly dog that looks at you with dulled eyes, refuses to eat and is in severe pain in spite of medication for its incurable condition, you may have an open discussion with your vet about relieving your dog's suffering by putting him down.

Relatives, friends and work colleagues with whom I discussed the issue of assisted dying were unanimous in their wish to have a right to die when they would like; and, if diagnosed with a terminal condition, they would want to have as open a discussion with their doctor for themselves as they could with their vet regarding their pets.

Euthanasia of animals, however, is not limited to those in pain with a terminal disease. It includes the destruction of animals in order to prevent their suffering and to control animal diseases that cause them significant pain as well as damage to the country's economy. In these ways, animal euthanasia goes beyond the scope of assisted dying in people. Concerns that there will be a broadening of the boundaries of assisted dying are at the heart of resistance to its legalisation in the UK.

I found it distressing to put unwanted animals to sleep. But the boxes of kittens brought to us were probably luckier than others in the manner of death they faced. The nurses would place them in a warm kennel with catnip toys, kitten food and a card on the door marked 'PTS' and one of the vets would eventually steel themselves to do so. And while it was upsetting to destroy greyhounds, past their racing peak and unsuitable for breeding or re-homing, the ones we saw were probably more fortunate than those that were euthanased in other ways. This explains why vets end up owning numerous cats and dogs; the ones they keep are a form of atonement for putting so many others to sleep.

Someone may find they can't afford to keep an older horse requiring long-term expensive medicines. And if searches for another home are fruitless, rather than see it abandoned or lacking in the care it needs, I would far rather it were humanely destroyed.

The usual fare for veterinary pathologists comprises animal carcasses, but occasionally our sense of smell was blessed with a live animal considered to have the condition affecting the herd or flock it came from. This gave us more information as we could examine them – watch them move, listen to their heart and lungs, take blood samples – and then after euthanasia open them up to get to the root of the problem and so treat and prevent the disease in other animals.

Because animal notifiable diseases, like Aujeszky's disease and Foot and Mouth Disease, threaten animal welfare and have serious economic consequences, we control them by slaughtering the infected ones and those that have been in contact with them. This is hard for farmers to accept and, when I arrived at their farms with a slaughter team, I didn't blame them for making me as welcome as a hog roast at a vegan barbecue. You take their life's work with their animals' lives and by the time you're washing and disinfecting your boots then heading home in your car, years of conscientious and devoted husbandry have been obliterated with a humane killer and pithing rod.

Understanding the requirement for slaughter of entire herds or flocks doesn't make it easy to do, either, and even though you ensure each animal dies humanely, this can be unpleasant for people exposed to it.

Martin, our senior veterinary officer, comes out of the farm house and walks, head down, towards us. He's no slim-jim and his white disposable boiler suit gives him a profile as global as the influence he appears to be aiming for at work. A tonsure of ginger curly hair encircles his scalp and his glasses are falling off his freckly nose where a blob of snot tries to escape.

'Right,' he says and sniffs. 'Aujeszky's disease has been confirmed on this farm. I've explained this to the farmer. We'll start culling in the farrowing houses now. The slaughter team are due to arrive shortly and will deal with the pigs from weaning upwards.'

We walk to the first farrowing house and open the door. The first sensation on entering such a place is the warmth – baby pigs must be kept at around 23°C. The next is the piggy smell mixed with the dusty, dried milk odour of piglet feed. Then you notice the peace, the maternal bliss of the sows lying on their sides in the farrowing crates, surrendering their bounteous udders to a group of ten or so pink, naked little souls. Just like your toes on the end of your foot, the piglets line up in parallel facing the udder, their tiny mouths around the teats, sucking and slurping and head-butting the udder to encourage more milk to flow. Nursing my own babies in years to come, I'll remember this place and feel a greater kinship than ever to these intelligent animals.

We work quietly. Communicate with head and hand movements. Everyone knows their role. It's a new one for me, called in from the veterinary laboratory service to help with the outbreak. I knew nothing about restriction notices and infected premises and control zones and I've had to make a brutal transition to whole-herd slaughter from my comfort zone of post mortem examinations.

Tom, a newly-recruited technical officer with straight brown hair covering his ears giving him a hippy look, steps in beside the first litter of pigs. He picks up a piglet and hands it to Eleanor who holds it on the floor in front of me. I make the lethal injection into the piglet. Eleanor lifts the tiny, warm carcase and places it respectfully outside the door. A technical officer with years of experience, she has a small herd of Gloucester Old Spot pigs which, due to the outbreak of Aujezsky's disease, she hasn't seen in weeks.

We go through the litters, piglet after piglet, overseen by Martin. By the time we have euthanased all the litters, the sows are standing up, snorting, grunting, squealing. They bite the bars of the farrowing crate, scrape the floor with their hooves and bang their heads against the bars above. Inchoate lives have been driven from neonatal utopia to oblivion while the pile of warm carcasses grows with the noise of the sows.

I watch Martin looking at the sows and catch his gaze for a second. He looks away and walks towards the farrowing house door, opens it then turns round. 'I'll ask the slaughtermen to come in now.'

We stand outside and take a breather. Eleanor takes the band from her long brown pony tail, smooths her hair, ties the band around it again, then exhales a mist through rounded lips.

I rub my quivering arms. The November cold feels much worse after being in the warmth of a porcine nursery and my ears are ringing with the sows' high-pitched squealing. I help Tom put the piglets we've euthanased into bags.

'You okay?' I ask him.

He shrugs. 'Didn't expect to be doing this. I thought I'd be saving animals' lives in this job.'

'But you are saving animals' lives in the long run,' I say, then grimace at my platitude.

Tom gives a half smile.

I inhale deeply. There's something about the smell of pigs that never leaves you. It lurks around your nasal passages, creeps osmotically into your skin and through each hair strand, and soap is as effective as a bucket to shift water in a sinking ship.

Martin returns.

'Right,' he says and sniffs, 'the slaughtermen are ready for the sows in this farrowing house. Let's get on with the litters in the next.'

'Can we wait just another minute?' Eleanor asks.

'Who would want to live to a hundred and three in a nursing home anyway?' the voice of a campaigner for assisted dying argued over the radio as I sat with my friend Pat drinking tea in her kitchen.

The electric kettle was bringing more water to the boil for the teapot, the AGA being turned off for the summer, when Pat frowned at the radio and shouted back.

'Someone who's a hundred and two.'

Her walls celebrated a lively and lengthy family history; pictures of herself astride a BSA B31 motorbike;

as a child with her pet donkey; her grandchildren with their children; a Pekingese curled up on a footstool. Normally, I felt chilly in the enormous stone house built over a hundred years ago. Still with the original pipes and radiators that stood like cold monuments, their function was replaced by twenty first century versions and a new boiler Pat got for free as part of a government scheme. But that day, her kitchen offered a cool sanctuary against the 25-degree June heat.

I smiled at her and nodded.

At the age of seventy, Pat started an animal sanctuary. In ten years, she had secured its charitable status and kept over ninety animals; horses as well as the pigs, donkeys and chickens taken to her for refuge. A cat heard about her and moved into her hay barn, earning his keep in vermin control.

Then, at eighty-seven, Pat broke her hip.

'You need to be mobile with the zimmer and have someone at home before you can leave,' the hospital ward staff ordered two weeks after her operation.

I nodded at her bedside, as did she, her white curls rising over her pink scalp. But her acquiescence belied her thoughts.

Two rows of white beds filled the lino-floored ward, a table at the end of each bed with a cardboard sick bowl, medicine bottles and maybe a copy of the Daily Record. The purposefulness of nurses, physiotherapists and doctors contrasted with the shrivelled, grey-skinned souls asleep, mouths open, toothless, or sitting up with nothing else to do but stare in front of them and wait. Open windows did their best to drag out the pungencies of hospital fish pie and vomit.

Pat escaped by exaggerating the help she had at home, in reality amounting to her chihuahua and mobile phone, and by purchasing an off-road mobility scooter that would have been the envy of Michael Dunlop.

A week or two later, fortified with her paracletes of Earl Grey, Soreen and Lurpak, she worked from morning until long after staff half her age had gone home, obliterating mutiny from her hip with Brufen and a nip of Balvenie.

Pat is not alone. There are many elderly and frail people, some who may be in pain yet continue to enjoy life's challenges, who celebrate their successes, accept their failures and keep their ambitions and dreams teenage-fresh, their lives still a work in progress. Queen Elizabeth II, 'in post' and working hard in her ninety-fifth year, is also amongst a population of older people who show that a fulfilling, active life is not mutually exclusive with advancing age which, therefore, need not be the driver to bring forward one's death.

Legal and ethical powers to assist someone's death will not make it straightforward. In the case of those with total dementia, even if they have provided an advance directive asking for their lives to be ended should they reach this state, we may not know whether they are happy and content and no longer wish to die before nature determines. Furthermore, due to the cost of assisted dying compared to treatment, those with terminal diseases may be encouraged to accept an assisted death rather than treatment.

For those in agony and wishing for an assisted death,

their relatives or doctors may find that, even if within the law, they cannot bring themselves to assist. I do not know whether, even if I were in unremitting, progressive and incurable agony, I would have the courage to end my own life. But I feel sure I do not have the emotional detachment necessary to help another human being to die; to hand them a lethal substance, lift it to their lips.

I doubt I am alone amongst my colleagues in finding that after giving a lethal injection, when the animal was dead, when there was no going back, all my measured reasons for euthanasia evaporated from my mind. Replacing them was the devil's advocate, lurking on my shoulder and snorting into my ear accusations of an absence of reverence for life.

When it came to discussing euthanasia of a pet animal with its owner, I was aware that in many cases the decision the owner made depended on what I said to them. Professionally, this was defensible: my obligation to ensure the animal's welfare informed the decision to euthanase. But from the point of view of our humanity, I wonder whether we should endow ourselves with authority over whether animals live or die, and I'm not sure, therefore, whether we are equipped to make the same decisions for ourselves.

To make legislative and ethical changes allowing assisted dying may bring as many problems as it provides solutions and may inflict as much suffering as the suffering it brings to an end. But I am sure of this: the taking of animals' lives comes with an emotional cost and, notwithstanding my certainty that it was in their best interests, it is one that I continue to pay.

9

CATCH ME IF YOU CAN:
AN ALPHABETISED MEDITATION ON IMITATION

ALEKSANDR ORLOV

Orlov, whose catchphrase 'simples' became legendary, is a fictional meerkat. Moreover, he is anthropomorphic, an animal ascribed with human appearances, feelings and behaviours, which probably explains his autobiography and his large following on social media.

BATES, H.W.

Some tasty animals look identical to those that are poisonous, so predators steer clear of the palatable ones.

Zoologists named this Batesian mimicry after their colleague who first described it. You can see this in harmless yellow and black flies resembling wasps and the edible African swallow-tail butterfly, which mimics some toxic species.

CLANCE, PAULINE

A psychology professor in Georgia, USA, Clance observed in the 1970s how some able students felt that they were frauds and that their success was due to chance or deceiving others into thinking they were talented.

Clance termed the condition 'Imposter syndrome'.

DRONGOS

When songbird drongos, the consummate con artists of the Kalahari, see meerkats with food, they mimic the alarm call of the meerkats who then run off, leaving their meal for the drongos. Simples.

ERSATZ

As wheat supplies dwindled during the Second World War, the Germans, with Teutonic resourcefulness, created ersatzbrot, a bread substitute made from potatoes and horse chestnuts.

Regarded as unavoidable anathema, this 'war bread' was tolerated by British Prisoners of War, as much as the ersatzkaffee, a hot beverage made from roasted beechnuts and acorns. My father, a POW in Poland, was grateful for this fake coffee as it warmed his hands and empty stomach.

FRANK ABAGNALE

In his late teens, Abagnale deceived everyone when he posed as an airline pilot, doctor and then parish prosecutor. But it was in the art of cheque fraud that he became so accomplished that the FBI asked for his help in tracking down other forgers.

GENUINE NOVICE RIDE

'Only one thing worse than a chestnut mare,' Charlie, my farrier, advised as he struggled to put shoes on my fiesty thoroughbred.

'What's that?' I asked.

'A red-headed woman,' Charlie replied.

'Why's that?'

Scarlett ripped her hind hoof out of Charlie's hands then bit his bottom.

'That's why,' he said.

He was right about the mare, sold to me as suitable for a novice rider. I never found her brakes and fell off more times than she booted and bit farriers. But I wondered what Charlie's red-heads did.

HORRORS OF EXAMS

I'm waiting in the exam hall lobby with other students. They're talking about things I don't understand and give each other calm and confident nods. My chest tightens, my heart throbs like a woodpecker and under my armpits my shirt feels damp.

I find a desk, sit down and look at the exam paper. There is not one question I can answer. I look around. Everyone has started to write with the fervour of a car parking attendant issuing a penalty notice. My breakfast fights to see the light of day again. Running out of the hall, I trip and wake up.

IMPOSTER (ɪmˈpɒstə)

noun: a person who pretends to be someone else.

JOAN OF ARC

The Maid of Orléans cropped her hair, dressed in men's clothes then led the French army to victory over the English in the 15th century. Later, she was captured and burned at the stake for witchcraft, heresy and pretending to be a man.

KASSANDRA

During the Trojan war, the Greeks built a wooden horse big enough to hide several armed warriors and offered it as a gift to the Trojans.

The daughter of King Priam of Troy, Kassandra, whose name became synonymous with someone whose truths are considered lies, warned that the gift would bring the city's downfall. Priam didn't believe her. He brought the Trojan horse inside the city walls and at night Greek warriors crept out of the horse, opened the city gates and let in the Greek army which then destroyed Troy.

LEWY BODY DEMENTIA

In the 1993 film Mrs Doubtfire, Robin Williams's character adopts the persona of a Scottish nanny, Mrs Euphegenia Doubtfire.

Using a mask, tweed skirt and woolly stockings he convinces his estranged wife to hire him to care for their children and fools everyone until his son catches him standing up to pee.

Robin Williams committed suicide in 2014. He was suffering from Lewy body dementia where abnormal proteins accumulate in brain cells, changing sufferers' personality and behaviour.

MILK SNAKES

If you're the cold and slimy sort of pet keeper rather than the warm and furry kind, get a milk snake. Their bright orange, yellow and tan bodies will add colour to your vivarium.

They get their name from the fable where a snake slips into a milking stall to sip from the cows' udders. This is impossible as snakes have no lips and can't sip but milk snakes survive in the wild by having the same colours as the venomous corral head snake. (See Batesian mimicry).

NOT A NORMAL VET

'Where does your mum work, Harriet?' I overheard the pale-faced child with blue tracking braces across her incisors ask my daughter as I tidied up one Saturday in the room next to them.

'Oakbank,' Harriet replied.

'Didn't know there's a vet's practice there,' Harriet's friend slurped behind the wires.

'There isn't,' Harriet said. 'Mum's not that sort of vet.'

'What sort is she then?'

'It's to do with laws and going to meetings.'

'Doesn't sound like vet work.'

'It is,' Harriet answered. 'Just not like a normal vet.'

ORLA

A boss I once had brought his pets to the veterinary practice for safe-keeping while he holidayed with his family. Bruce the Boxer blitzed the biscuit boxes; Whistler and Forbes, white-furred felines, whined all day and Orla, the mynah bird spat with the regularity and volume of a smoker with consumption.

But Orla redeemed herself with mimicking. The bird, adopting the boss's Norfolk brogue and his wife's posh Glaswegian, gave us intimate details of their domestic routines, worth more than the sticks of rock they brought back.

PIG DAY

'Today, Sheilagh Nisbet, from the state veterinary service, will give a lecture on pig diseases,' Professor Taylor introduced me to the fourth year Glasgow vet students.

The students opened their laptops and began to type.

The professor continued. 'Sheilagh has a post-graduate qualification in pig medicine…'

…*by sheer luck that I got examiners who liked my coltish legs and yellow hair. Nothing whatsoever to do with my ability.*

An ice-cube-like shiver dripped down my spine.

I know nothing about pigs…

'…so she is well-placed to share her knowledge and first hand experience in exotic pig diseases.'

I've seen swine fever, that's all. And I've never seen foot and mouth disease in pigs. Except in the experimental unit. I know little more than these students. Goodness, they look bright.

I tore a tissue in my jacket pocket into pieces then reached for the glass of water on the table beside me.

'Sheilagh has brought with her a range of preserved specimens…'

… but I've forgotten what they're supposed to show – which one is swine vesicular disease? I've no right to be here.

The water left my mouth dry.

'…and will be pleased to answer your questions in the time available at the end of the lecture.'

No. Please. No questions. Not from these fiendishly intelligent kids. They'll catch me out.

'So, I'll hand over to Sheilagh.'

My knee caps shivered like jellyfish on a Scottish seashore. I steadied each with a molten hand then breathed, stood up and walked towards the gallows-like lectern.

QUACK

'I'll cut into your scrotum,' John Brinkley said to the man palpitating on the examination couch, 'then insert a goat's testicle beside your own.'

'Will that work, Doc?' the man asked, spewing fear from every pore.

Brinkley adjusted his spectacles then smoothed his goatee beard coiffured to perfection.

'Never known to fail,' he replied, shuffling a shiny cufflink.

With his trademark self-importance Brinkley, an American fake doctor, began the operation, one he did on hundreds of impotent men, promising them brio in their bedrooms.

RIP-OFF

The vernacular for fraud. As a verb it means to take credit for something that you didn't do, as those of us with imposter syndrome do all the time.

STEVEN SPIELBERG

In 1997 the film rights to Frank Abagnale's autobiography were sold to Spielberg's DreamWorks and the biographical crime film, 'Catch me if you can', was released in 2002 starring Leonardo DiCaprio.

TROJAN HORSE

Vets were puzzling over how the bovine viral diarrhoea (BVD) virus spread. They'd advise farmers not to buy cattle with antibodies to BVD, but still their herds got disease.

Then healthy calves dubbed 'Trojan horses' were discovered, little bovines bearing the innocence of seraphim and without antibodies to BVD. Yet their bodies tolerated and so were hooching with BVD virus. They handed this out to herd-mates with the generosity of leaflet-distributing Jehovah's witnesses, bringing pestilence and death wherever they coughed and sneezed, pooped and pee'd.

UROFOLLITROPIN

My ovaries produced no eggs. This was fine, as it brought a hormonal homogeneity that spared me from the interloping cyclical depredation that turns your brain to vapour and body to bloated blubber, as some of my fertile contemporaries suffered. Fine until I hoped for, then yearned for, then mourned for not being able to have, children.

Enter by subcutaneous injection urofollitropin, a hormone that gives one's ovaries the output of a prize-winning pullet at her peak. Over the next eight years I, the mother who wasn't supposed to be, gave birth six times.

VETERINARY QUACK

A South African, Peter Keniry posed as a vet by borrowing the identity of a member of the Royal College of Veterinary Surgeons and secured locum positions in small animal practices in England.

Practice staff commented that he did well enough, while he attributed his 'rustiness' to a recent holiday. Keniry had received thousands of pounds in wages before his fraud was discovered and punished with a custodial sentence.

WILMUT, IAN

Professor Sir Ian Wilmut led the group at Edinburgh University that first cloned a sheep from an adult cell. Hitherto, unlike plants capable of the less complicated production of a new plant simply by budding one off from themselves, mammals had to indulge in the fraught and uncertain business of sexual reproduction in which you just never know what you'll end up with.

However, the prospect of extending this to humans brought concerns and congratulations in equal measure: while potentially bringing fertility to the infertile and uniform disease resistance to the universe, how would we prevent the production of populations of AntiChrists? Cloning is so unnatural, too. And no one else would know which one was you, the original you, the real you, and which was your clone.

XIPHOPHORUS

Female Xiphophorus, swordtail fish, prefer to mate with males whose tail is elongated into a sword, rather than the hapless males with a blunt-ended tail.

When zoologists fitted plastic swords to a group of blunt-tailed swordfish males, females were fooled into mating with the prosthesis-carrying males as often as those with real sword tails.

YOUNG, DR

'Come in, Mrs Thomas,' I said to the twin-setted, multi-pearled lady with one cat basket in the waiting room.

'Bertha' Thomas was my first consult. My first ever as a new graduate. No vet next door to oversee and supervise and save me from myself.

Mrs Thomas walked to the consulting table cradling her cat basket then put it down as if she were putting an infant to bed.

'What can I do for you and Bertha today?' I asked.

'I'll wait for Dr Young,' Mrs Thomas replied elevating a Lancôme'd chin and nose.

'Well, actually,' I said, fiddling with the stethoscope in the pocket of my virginally-white coat, 'Dr Young isn't here today. May I help you?'

'It's a vet I need,' she said with self-righteous rhetoric.

'Of course. And I am one.'

She looked at me like a stain on Axminster. 'You? A vet?' she said, her pearls rising with her cashmere-encased bosom. 'You look no more than fifteen. I want to see a proper vet.' She shook her shampoo-and-set. 'I doubt you can help us at all.'

She picked up the basket and left.

Mrs Thomas was right. I had a piece of paper that said I was a Bachelor of veterinary medicine and surgery. I had another piece of paper that proclaimed me a member of the Royal College of Veterinary Surgeons. I had no experience and I had a blank mind. I knew nothing about cats. I knew nothing about anything.

ZEN WITH ZABAGLIONE

'Why are vets anxious?' asked Matt, my fellow pig vet.

We'd finished an Italian tour, to investigate producing Parma ham back in Peterborough, with lunch in a Turin restaurant as languid as the Vatican.

'We're perfectionists. When we make a mistake, we feel fake,' I replied. 'Mindfulness helps, I'm told.'

Our zabaglione arrived, a dish with the benign appearance of egg custard but with a David Beckham kick.

'This, too?' Matt asked.

We tucked in, and as the Marsala reached its neuronal goals, we resolved to try a little Zen.

10

NOT GRAZING BUT BROWSING

Fenella Macdonald, a television presenter is kneeling on the grass beside me. Tyler, a member of the film crew, his hair shaved off his head at the back and sides, points a microphone like a priapic bull rush above us. The untattooed parts of Tyler's exposed skin are knitted together with metal.

Dominic, the cameraman, adjusts a Lilliputian piece of equipment on his shoulder. A man of generous proportions, he walks as if wading through treacle and I see he's wearing these plastic shoes with holes in the top that make them look like a shower head.

'Okay, we're all set,' he calls out.

'From Skyros to Scotland,' Fenella pauses as she turns away from the camera to gaze with the love of a new mother at the wee bay mare next to her. Looking back to the camera, she gushes, 'Treasured by Alexander the Great as he set out to conquer Persia, these little horses are now flourishing in Scotland thanks to the enthusiasm of a small group of keepers.'

Fenella completes her introduction, serene in front of the camera and cashing in on her photogenicity and posh Scottish accent. She's wearing a light pink polo shirt with an expensive-looking logo and aubergine chinos hug her shapely posterior.

She turns to me and flashes her pearly whites while giving a coquettish swish of her auburn tresses. 'So, Sheilagh, how did you hear about these little horses?'

I'd ruled out telling the whole truth about how I became a producer of this rare Greek breed. It could be summarised as a lesson in the consequences of following your heart and ignoring common sense as obvious as the piles of poo created by working stallions. But that wouldn't make good telly.

'Well,' I look towards Fenella's perfect complexion, 'I set out to buy another moorland pony but the breeder, John Carter, showed me the Skyrians instead.'

*

Five years earlier, I'd met John in the yard outside his house and he responded to my self-introduction with a 'hello' that sounded more like a growling going over. With him were about half a dozen girls, all with a pony at livery there. Later, they told me they each paid £15 per week, which seemed cheap until I witnessed the various chores John, not unreasonably, perhaps, asked them to do: move these ponies; mend this fence; fill the hay racks; put the kettle on.

We all jumped into John's well-used and superannuated Land Rover. I was in the front, amongst nails, bits of fence wire, bailer twine and about twenty years of mud. John's stomach, bursting out between the strangled buttons of his shirt, barely fitted behind the steering wheel. His sparse, white hair, plastered down with something shiny, contrasted with his stubbled face and he spoke like a sub machine gun.

'All these foals have been sold,' he announced as he drove past a group of Fell and Dartmoor mares with their offspring, long legs and little else.

He stopped the Land Rover to let the students out. 'What do you want with that?' he demanded of them.

'It's ointment for Primrose, John,' one of the girls answered, 'she has a cut above one of her fetlocks.'

I was thankful to be behind his head when he shouted, 'It's a field lameness. Doesn't need it. Leave it alone.'

He muttered as he turned to look through the windscreen, his eyebrows forming a deep V shape, 'Stupid girls.'

We got out of the Land Rover and as he led me down the hill, I could see he moved with considerable pain.

*

A colt frisking my pocket for carrots brings me back to Fenella. 'Why did you decide to breed these horses, Sheilagh?'

Why indeed. Why would anyone want to expand the global numbers of a horse that is rare because, in plain English, few people want to buy it. Trying to remove the colt from my pocket gives me time to compose a response, a bit like taking a sip of water when you get the ridiculous question in a job interview, 'if you were an animal what would you be?'

I think how this wee horse reflects the Greek people's history and development over many years, how invaluable to Skyrian cereal producers they were before tractors and combine harvesters came to the island and wonder whether I should argue that their horses, therefore, are as worthy of preservation as the Parthenon.

Or I could mention how the feral Skyros horses contribute to global equine diversity, and how they live on the Vouno of Skyros, the rugged mountainous southerly areas of the island, showing they have the genes to survive and multiply on sparse, poor quality feed, with little water and in extremes of temperature. And how the breed is therefore a genetic resource that may not be in demand now but as climates and production systems evolve, there may come a requirement for what it offers. After all, the Greeks wouldn't abandon the Parthenon because it wasn't currently fit for purpose due its lack of damp proofing and double glazing and a leak-proof roof.

But I'm not sure these arguments are relevant to a short tea-time TV feature or the sort of issues likely to inspire a conversation with Fenella.

I pull the colt's head from deep in my coat. 'John Carter's health was deteriorating and he didn't feel up to the increasing demands of the herd. So he asked me to continue the breeding programme,' I say, trying to sound as if I'd been awarded a Nobel prize.

*

John had told me about his sciatica as we walked towards a paddock surrounded by hawthorn bushes and chewed wooden fencing. I admired his courage for his continuing equine enthusiasms while suffering chronic pain.

He stopped by a metal gate where the buckles and bends in the bars made it look like a drawing of the London Underground and asked, 'What do you think these horses are?'

I looked at a dozen or so wee souls with prominent ribs that contrasted with the spring grass roundness of John's moorland ponies. The only generous parts to the former were their thick, long manes and tails and their slightly pendulous abdomens. Their brown or bright bay coats, all with a black stripe along the spine, reflected the June sun but the raggedness of the hoof horn suggested John had struggled to keep on top of foot care.

'Well, they're fine limbed but with primitive markings and colours. Part Arab, part Fell?' I guessed.

John's face suggested that he was striving not to point out I was as stupid as the girls.

'They're Skyrian ponies from the Greek island of Skyros,' he gruffed.

'Oh,' I said, 'but they're quite horse-shaped, aren't they? Insofar as they are as tall as they are long, I mean.'

'They're ponies,' he expostulated.

John's look told me that this was not a theory proffered for discussion but a statement of fact.

'They're a bit on the lean side,' I dared to comment.

John shrugged. 'There are a few a lot leaner on Skyros. Come inside and I'll show you a video about them.'

Along with hoof care, John appeared to be struggling with house keeping. The furniture, pictures, ornaments and television were dusty and the floors looked unacquainted with a vacuum cleaner. The armchairs would have been an enthusiastic re-upholsterer's dream.

I asked to use the bathroom. I walked down the dim hallway where cobwebs formed hammocks between the walls and covered the cornices. Near doorways, the carpet consisted of threads held together by mud.

In the sitting room John was loading an old video player. I declined his offer of coffee, although I needed caffeine.

'Your daughter?' I asked, pointing to a faded photograph in an elegant frame of a girl about ten years old wearing a light blue shirt, navy tie and grey cardigan with yellow stripes on the edges. She had long, dark, wavy hair and her smile to the camera revealed slightly protruding front teeth with a gap between them.

John nodded while he turned on the TV. He sat down as the video started with some footage of sparkling white buildings alongside a shoreline met with a brilliant green sea.

'This is Skyros,' he said without looking at me. 'She's thirty-five now. A teacher in Newcastle,' he said as we continued to watch the video.

'You must be proud of her,' I suggested.

He nodded.

*

Fenella's interest in my project appears authentic and I begin to warm to her as we move away from the doubtful logic of my breeding programme.

'What were the Skyrians used for originally?' she asks patting the stallion's neck as if his skin were a hot plate.

Ivan lifts his elegant Skyros head, looks at her down his long muzzle and snorts.

'Mostly corn threshing and traction until they were replaced by mechanisation in the 1960s. Now they are used as children's mounts,' I assert, handing Fenella a tissue from my pocket to wipe away Ivan's spittle from her cheek, while remembering John's old video and the scenes of a sparsely-covered landscape with ponies to match.

The boss mare of the herd pushes her hindquarters into Fenella's side, knocking the shapely presenter off balance.

'It's her way of asking you to scratch her bum,' I explain, helpfully.

Fenella obliges until she breaks a nail. 'And what else are they used for now?' she asks, staring at her ruined manicure.

Ah. Another one as tricky as the job interview question, 'if you were a felt tip pen which colour would you be?'

If the Skyros had multiple uses, of course, they wouldn't be rare. The market is small for an equine breed with so small a stature that you have to be under 40kg to ride it.

'Well,' I respond, helping Fenella out with scratching the boss mare's bum, 'they're docile and sweet-natured horses so ideal for equine-assisted therapies.'

Fenella raises her eyebrows.

'You know, using horses to help with various physical therapies and also some forms of psychotherapy. Horses help people get in touch with their feelings,' I explain.

Fenella nods as her eyebrows descend.

'They make good companions, too. And they're brilliant biological lawn mowers,' I add, making her smile and maybe forgetting for a minute the defilement of her nail and cheek.

*

'This is the Vouno,' John explained, 'where some of the ponies are turned out to fend for themselves in winter.'

The rest of the video gave an account of how some of the Skyros people began to cross breed the ponies to make them bigger and improve their conformation. I sympathised with this. John condemned it. We had chosen different sides of the arguments over breeding pure and outcrossing.

If pure bred animals of a breed are not maintained, we may lose the genetic resource they offer, while cross breeding gives the progeny hybrid vigour so they grow more vigorously, they're more athletic and their wider utility gives them an economic value. The first cross would also create a further use for the pure bred animal, of course, but I sensed that continuing this debate with John would be as exhausting and fruitless as spring cleaning his house.

I got up to go, thanking him for his time and looking forward to some fresh air. As I left him at his door, he forbade me from telling anyone about the Skyrians in case gypsies stole them. I gave him the assurances he needed, at the same time wondering how he could establish a market for them if they were kept a secret.

It was a few days later when John rang to say that he knew of someone selling a Fell colt. 'Or,' he added, 'would you be interested in taking the Skyrians?'

He went on to explain, with a tangible sadness, that besides the worsening sciatica, he had arthritis and the herd was becoming too much for him. I was taken aback with his kindness and felt honoured he was willing to entrust me with his Skyrian project.

*

'So you brought all the Skyrians to your holding here,' Fenella states the obvious while inviting me to offer some entertaining back story.

Should I tell her about my first summer with the Skyrians when they not only lawnmowered the entire three paddocks but carried out some effective tree surgery too. Not grazing but browsing, as it happened. Or the first autumn before I was blessed to meet Rosemary Dale of the Scottish Borders Donkey Sanctuary, and her daughter Sandra Harrison, two exceptional women who found other breeding partners to look after some of the ponies. About the severe snows that winter which made poo picking impossible and amplified hay consumption to a level that must have been equivalent to the horses of the entire Household Cavalry. The time that would have been all mud, glaur, head-in-hands, what-the-hell-have-I-done, had it not been for my enjoyment in caring for these sweet little souls and their Fell paddock mate.

But I make do with a nod to summarise the ball and chain of events that led to my ownership of the herd.

'I was new to horse breeding, though, so I had a steep learning curve ahead. I visited other breeders to find out about their methods,' I say with the inquisitiveness of the team aboard Apollo 11.

*

It was true that, with an earnestness for my vocation that would match Buzz Aldrin's, I set out to learn the ropes, starting with a visit to a breeder of a similar small horse, the Caspian. I'd heard that the saving of this breed had been a success story. Thought to have become extinct, it was rediscovered by an American, Louise Firouz, on the Southern shores of the Caspian Sea in Northern Iran, as she looked for small horses for her riding school in Tehran. With a programme of selective breeding, she produced a horse with elegant proportions, movement and conformation and a good all-rounder suitable for mounted games, gymkhanas, driving and show jumping.

I arrived at Rhoda's farm full of optimism and enthusiasm and she showed me around her thirty or so horses.

'What sort of prices do you get for them?' I asked as we stood in a shed, paint peeling off the doors and walls, although the horses in stables along either side of the passageway all looked very bright and in good condition, as they munched away happily on their hay nets.

Rhoda turned to me and began to cry. 'I haven't sold anything for over two years. We're in a bit of a downturn.'

Rhoda's demeanour, along with her buildings, confirmed a current lack of market for small horses, and I left with a heart as heavy as the dung heap that she was waiting to get collected.

Clinging to the straws of hope, I rang another Caspian breeder to check out Rhoda's gloomy predicament.

'We've just got to batten down the hatches. Secure the tarpaulins,' Steven replied with lyrical, if discouraging, tropes. 'Keep going until sales pick up again.'

Nonetheless, I pressed on and, with the help of my breeding partners who shared my gullibility and belief that one day the Skyrian would be as sought after as rhino horn, expanded the herd from fourteen to thirty. I felt I had to put to one side John's warnings about gypsies and set out to raise the profile of the breed such that nearly a dozen people in Scotland had become familiar with them. This would continue to grow after the TV programme, of course, when I'd have recruits queuing to the Skyros cause.

*

'And what was it about the Skyrian that drew you to them, Sheilagh?'

Fenella's question reminds me of the task in hand and I look for inspiration in her dark eyelashes as long as a newborn foal's. She flutters them encouragingly.

'Well, besides wanting to help maintain and promote them, I found their unusual appearance intriguing,' I say, using this euphemism for their non-conforming conformation, 'and you can see their gentle temperaments.'

I add this persuasiveness, as Dominic sweeps the camera to my treasures nibbling a wing mirror of Fenella's exquisite 4x4.

'And blood tests have confirmed how unique their DNA is.' I feel sure this will provide a convincing slant to my argument, 'research carried out by …'

'Stop,' commands Dominic, stepping into a pile of soft pony poo, 'we don't want that big one in the background.'

I turn to see my Fell shuffle across the paddock behind me. We wait until he's out of shot, by which time both Fenella and I have forgotten where we were. She quickly recovers; she's a professional after all.

'Are they good as children's ponies,' she says more as a viewer-drawing statement, and with an implicit wanting to be somewhere, anywhere, other than the nerve centre of the Scottish Skyrian herd.

They make excellent children's ponies I say, but when Dominic puts his camera down and asks me for a stick to clean the holes in his shoe, the crew decide they've seen enough.

11

Hog Couture:
A PERUSAL OF SARTORIAL FUNCTIONS

CLOTHES THAT CONFORM

I've hated wearing skirts, ever since I remember. They remove every last molecule of what makes me me. If I had been born forty years later in the 1990s when trousers were an acceptable item of school uniform for girls, my early life would have been transformed. Dressed in white, square-neck blouse, gymslip and cardigan with ridiculous three-quarter length sleeves, I never initiated conversation with anyone, spoke only when spoken to and wondered around the playground on my own. But dressed in my play trousers, trainers and T shirt I walked tall, inter-reacted with peers, and felt equal to everyone.

One of the most uncomfortable days of my life to date was when, at the age of six, maybe seven, I had to be a bridesmaid at my cousin Phyllis's wedding. I loathed the frilly, frilly, itchy, itchy dress, the tiny ankle socks and shiny dolly T-bar shoes and, worst of all, that my hair was put into rags the night before so that my wedding look was completed with a blonde version of the barnet of the wee guy on the marmalade jar. Looking at my grimaces in all the pictures, I still recall the cold, discomfort and humiliation I felt throughout that day.

Another memorable occasion is as erasable from my memory as a greasy school dinner from the stomach. I'd followed my Granny Andrews as she puffed like an angry rhino up the stairs of her little terraced, two up two down, house in Leith. Her bottom filled my entire visual field and her bowed legs creaked, one after the other. She stepped onto the landing, breathing out like a cart horse.

'Aye, it's a sair fecht,' she said as she shook her head, grasping the bannister.

I joined her on the landing and nipped around her to go into the bedroom I was using while my parents, bother, sister and I were visiting.

'Look, Granny. See what I've bought to wear to Church tomorrow,' I said holding up my grey gaberdine chinos.

'Whit? Breeks? Ye canna wear breeks tae the Kirk, lassie. Wudna be richt. An' whaur's yer hat?'

'Don't want one, Granny.'

'A wummin canna gang intae a kirk wi' naethin on 'er heid. A'll awa' an get ye ane o' mine.'

'No, really, granny…'

'An' a pair o' gloves.'

She puffed into the bedroom next door and I followed, brow in folds, lips pressed together. As she opened her wardrobe, it exhaled napthalene. She rifled through the upper shelf and found a white, lacy hat and gloves to match.

'Ere. Pit them oan, lassie. Thu'll do fine, aye.'

'Granny, no. They won't fit me. I'll look daft in them.'

I turned and ran back to my bedroom. Granny followed and eventually arrived, a baleful eye on my 'floordrobe' and Donnie Osmond poster.

'Whit a sliaster yuv got this room intae. Wait till ah tell yer Dad.'

She turned around with the velocity of an oil tanker and yelled down the stairs.

'Rubburt! Rubburt! Will ye get yersel up here an' knock some sense intae this lassie o' yours. Shu'll no can gang tae the kirk withoot the richt clothes an' ye shud see the mess in 'er bedroom.'

CLOTHES TO LET YOU BE SOMEONE ELSE

Whether you're going to a party, raising money for charity or substituting for Santa Claus, wearing fancy dressing dress is no longer the province of the under tens at Halloween.

Rather than make do with a brightly-coloured tie that squirts water and blows raspberries, even men are embracing the whole concept and using fancy dress with abandon, allowing them to enjoy a bit of behavioural flexibility and explore parts of their identity they haven't felt able to express before.

Imagine how different you'd feel dressed up as Hitler instead of Mahatma Ghandi. It wouldn't be just the contrasting textures and thermal qualities of jack boots and jesus sandals – the former might make you feel powerful and self-righteous instead of endowing you with the altruism and philanthropy you'd get from the latter.

Enthusiasm for dressing up explains the success of Morphsuits, a company started by a few Edinburgh students in their spare time and producing onesies to transform you into Darth Vader, Spider Man or Donald Trump faster than clipping on a plastic nose with integral glasses and moustache. Dressed in head-to-toe colourful lycra, no longer do you spend all evening in the kitchen beside the empties, chicken bones and somnolent drunks and instead you become the proverbial life and soul, opening up conversations with people you've never met and moving around the crowd with the ease of an influenza virus. For just one evening you can be someone else, behave out of character, tap into your alter ego and no one will blink one censoring eye.

CLOTHES TO HELP YOU BE YOURSELF

My first flared denims came with the advent of my teenage years and a clothes allowance. Because this was frugal, I got a job in a local kennels to buy the matching jacket and shovelling dog poo for denim filled my weekends.

Rushing back from school, tearing off my blazer, blouse, pinafore and vestal white ankle socks, each item to a beat of *It's only Rock'n Roll*, I donned the denims, and the mirror confirmed my defiant boyish frame, just like Jagger's. With a splash of Goya *Meadowsong,* and a dab of Mary Quant blusher, I was set for the disco at the Church

Youth Fellowship group, the 'be back by eleven' wave from Dad acknowledged and ignored.

'Oh, it's Wee Moosy,' mocked Alistair, as I walked into the Manse's converted stables, decorated with posters of Snoopy and a tennis player scratching her bum.

Alistair was the minister's son and big brother of my sister Val's mate, Ann. Six foot something of fashionable lankiness was crowned with blond curtains across his blue eyes and I suppose there may have been an affectionate element in his nickname for me. After all, he was kind enough to play table football with my wee brother, Robin, on Wednesday evenings while our parents were at choir practice. Moreover, Alistair's flares were of such width and length he swept away snow with them but I knew he'd had more girlfriends than games of Subbuteo. Maybe he looked down on me in more than a literal sense, but when I caught him at the disco looking at my denim-clad butt, I grabbed Neville, he of the sautéed hair, chicken-pox face and baked bean body odour, and whirled around to the multi-coloured disco rhythms.

It was inevitable that Alistair was the first of us to wear loon pants, and it soon dawned on the rest of us that with this *de rigueur* garment, particularly if tie-dyed or batiked, the world was our loiter. Writing 'Jesus' on the right leg and 'is Lord' on the left leg in candle grease, then cold dying the yellow cotton black, resulted in a look as cheerful as a Leonard Cohen lyric, but I was bearing witness; spreading The Word.

'Do you want to swap, then?' a musty smelling stick insect from Glasgow's Summerhill asked me when we were at the Keswick Convention. Steven wrote the sort of deep and meaningful poetry that years later makes you screw your eyes and suck your teeth.

Maybe he liked me, but his loons fitted me better, and he couldn't do the batik thing because he did wood work at school, not crafts. When the Bible study groups got boring even for born-again Christians, we wondered round Keswick, in and out of middle-aged cake shops to avoid the rain and share a slice of tipsy cake, and when the mud at the campsite grew osmotically up the legs, we washed our loons by swimming in Windermere.

One of life's enigmas was that when I became a grant-dependant student my love for the hitherto unaffordable Levis was consummated. And I discovered, with the tribulations of a parent who has looked for forty years for an estranged child and finds they've been living in the next street, that Levis work out cheaper because they last longer and I wore my deep blue versions like military decorations. They embraced me in the right places and gave room to breathe in others; the dark colour didn't look dirty too soon so lasted until my fortnightly bag wash; they were flared but not with a loon-pant absurdity and I made sure my jumpers were never long enough to cover up the wee bit of leather on the waist band with the name in subdued red. This was for real; we were made for each other.

Levis and I continued our relationship into my working life, but only at weekends, as the workplace required smarter attire. I had hoped that Levi cords were the answer but found they gave me the sense of loss engendered by visiting a childhood haunt to find it buried by an NCP multi storey.

Then, just as I resigned myself to this part time love, succour came in the form of the black denim Levi 501; boot cut, button fly, things of beauty. The first day I wore them into work I walked around the blue-carpeted, file-lined office that smelled of cardboard, feeling the green eyes gazing at my butt and legs.

'Your jeans are so nice I hate you,' Nicola's face said and by the next Monday she had a pair. It was no time before Chris copied Nicola, and Dave copied Chris and the majority of the office was in black denim splendour.

To be on trend and a step ahead of the crowd, I moved on to the Levi 507 with the narrower leg and zipped fly. Now that the work-friendly Levi and I had discovered each other, I had no doubt that we would be together. Forever.

Our problems probably began with the engineered jeans. Even now, I can't make sense of Levi's decision to make jeans in a spiral cut that twisted round your legs like you've gone to sleep in them. As if that wasn't bad enough, the shape had transmogrified to fit curvy girls: big around the hips and thighs, tight at the waist was a style incompatible with my tubular frame.

I searched everywhere for the engineer that might fit and ordered parcel after parcel online, returning each of them and, with a sense of failure to match Shackleton's on the *Endurance*, I knew I'd lost. I longed for the halcyon days of our love, even wore my old 501s to try to enliven our fading relationship, but it simply wasn't working.

It wasn't long before my kids began to notice and ask questions.

'You know at school,' I began one Saturday over a McFlurry after swimming, 'when you're great friends with someone and then gradually you spend less time with them and more with other people?'

Harriet and Robbie looked at each other then at me, a slow nod from both.

'It's a bit like that with my Levis.'

We chose a seaside caravan in Bamburgh for the summer holidays. I wore my old 501s, the legs cut off to just below the knee and frayed, and hoped for the weather to justify it.

My *quid pro quo* to the kids for joining me in an edifying visit to Alnwick Castle was a day shopping in the Metro Centre. Dodging apathetic men and achromatic girls pushing buggies, we wondered into Debenhams where Robbie saw the Converse high tops she wanted for her birthday. This was four months away but, heck, it was the holidays and while Robbie tried on the trainers, my eyes wondered to the jeans rack. There they were, staring at me. Beckoning. Whispering.

'Try me on. Try. Me. On.'

I checked the labels, found my size, took them to a changing room and ten minutes later, we wondered into the sun blessed mall with the blue Converse, a bright green bomber jacket that Harriet liked and Pepe Jane.

'Be careful,' friends warned me, pointing to my Pepes when I returned to the office, 'are you sure about wearing them at work?'

I shrugged. 'Haven't had any complaints,' and underscored my conviction by taking the 507s to Oxfam.

They say that what happens on holiday should stay on holiday. But what began in a melanoid changing room in the north east's palace of hell mushroomed like nuclear fission. It took only days for Nicola to wonder in wearing blue denim, albeit in a sober dark wash. Chris copied Nicola, Dave copied Chris but Martin went even further with super skinny drainpipes and black Vans. Some said this was down to his divorce, but I maintained that if he'd ditched the cavalry twills and market boots earlier, Paula might have stayed.

'Well,' remarked Richard, our longest-serving admin assistant, as he reflected on my unanticipated promotion to a role hitherto the province of the male, pale and podgy, 'you'll certainly have the best bum we've ever seen in that job.'

The others gazed at their shoes, while I whispered thanks to my Pepe Venus straight leg.

CLOTHES TO CRIPPLE

I was looking for the pig farm where I'd arranged a visit somewhere in a late twentieth century bucolic billiard table. Beyond the fields with a patina of Passchendaele was a muddy estuary where the white horses were more like cappuccino froth and a large ship was fleeing towards the sea.

I drove past a graveyard with headstones like the mouth of a stranger to the dentist then glanced at my OS map with the red cross that I hoped wasn't far away.

Normally, the faecal smell of pigs in indirect proportion to my distance from a farm helped locate it but here the pig smell was as ubiquitous as fried onions in Blackpool. Then, out of nowhere and nailed to a tree I saw a piece of driftwood with a drawing of a pig and beneath it in red letters, 'Keep out.'

This was a high health farm referring not to the personnel's state of health, but to the pigs' and to keep them that way they banned visitors, with the exception of their vet and only then with the fondness of cats for swimming.

I parked up and hooted my horn. The farm manager, Frank, appeared from a building and we met either side of a fence, three metres high, encircling the pig farm. We exchanged greetings and comments on the fluctuations of the mercury.

'When and where were you last in contact with pigs?' Frank asked, opening a brown notebook with 'Visitors' scrawled on the front and 'Woolworths 1s 6d' written in the top right corner. His sparse hair gave his head the appearance of a spider plant and as he looked down to find the latest entry, I could see his white scalp was covered in freckles.

'Four days ago in Newtown,' I replied.

Frank nodded and as he wrote, I saw he had L O V E tattooed on the knuckles of his right hand.

He pointed towards a building at the perimeter fence. 'Go through the front door and take off all your clothes.'

I knew the drill, but he went over it anyway, as per the pig company's directions.

'Leave them in the cubicle, then go into the shower. You must wash thoroughly paying particular attention to body hair,' he said, staring at me, not a blink. 'Then go through the other side of the shower. There's a towel and some clothes for you. And, erm,' he held up a plastic bag with Tesco on the sides, 'there's some, erm, other things in here...,' he said, pulling out what I could see was a bra strap.

Not many of the pig units I visited provided clothing specifically for women, most clinging to times thirty years ago when visitors were only men. Frank didn't appear grateful for his employer's progressive stance.

Inside the shower block, I undressed and left my clothes in a concrete compartment with a wooden bench like a sixties swimming pool then walked into the shower.

The aim was to make sure you weren't bringing any organisms on your skin and hair harmful to the pigs, but I'd seen better showering facilities in the former Soviet Union and I wondered who might infect whom.

The wooden, slatted shower base was covered in a mucoid film that felt like pond slime and I had to fiddle the shower dial round to maximum for lukewarm water. I avoided further misery by averting my eyes from the walls where mould species flourished as on Stilton, used the litre-for-50p shampoo then, after freeing the bar of soap from curly, dark hairs, I washed as per Frank's instructions.

Stepping out of the shower, I walked towards the 'clean' side where I prayed a towel would be waiting rather than any of the pigmen. I exhaled when I saw the former, frayed and defiled but it would get me dry. Then I looked at a pile of clothes beside the Tesco's bag. However, it wasn't necessary to look through the latter as Frank had laid out a suggestion on top of the clothes – a fetching number in black lace. One melon-size cup would have served as a hat, so I replaced the garment and searched the bag for my more modest and humanly-possible 34A.

In the pile, I found boxer shorts with stains front and back and decided to go commando then forced my feet through the splints of socks. The men's XXL T-shirt, lilac but it may once have been white, and bearing the reassuring slogan, 'No Fear' was comfortable enough but the grey tracksuit bottoms reached my nipples and the sweatshirt fell off my right shoulder. No matter: I pulled on the overalls, with the crotch that reached my knees and turned each wellington boot upside down to check for mice and spiders before stepping into them.

'Everything okay for you?' Frank asked as I tramped into the farm office.

I caught his deputy, Ray, and another pigman, Kevin, exchange a smirk.

'Yes, thanks. All fine,' I replied, deadpan.

To complain may have underscored their apparent conviction that women made life difficult on a pig unit. But what we were all certain of was that the over-sized clothing made me feel vulnerable, put me on the back foot and gave me the confidence of a rat surrounded by Jack Russell Terriers.

My long hair, another symbol of the non-male, dripped onto my clipboard.

'May I see the herd performance records, please?' I asked Frank and as he rummaged through a drawer I glanced at the walls.

Surrounding a notice declaring that pig meat must not be consumed on the premises were pictures depicting a scale of pornography that I felt must be illegal in this country. It emphasised, gratuitously, that the only women welcome were those decorating the walls in naked and physically impossible poses for the entertainment of men, providing a distraction from their work while they munched through their pig-free meals.

Ray and Kevin smiled at each other. I lost my fight not to blush.

CLOTHES THAT UNCOVER TRADITIONALISTS

Post-mortem rooms are tile-covered places as welcoming as a public convenience. Iodine disinfectant fights trooper-like against the 360 degree odour of putrefaction and an array of knives that would be the envy of Heston Blumenthal glint in the retina-sizzling strip lights.

I was standing in cotton overalls, men's extra-small and enough for two of me, and a calf-length apron reaching my ankles. I plodded as if wearing snowshoes in my white boots, men's size six, and worked through the list of animals submitted for examination. Bright yellow rubber gloves were wearable but since my colleague, Dick, sliced half his thumb off while removing a bull's brain, we were required to wear chain mail gloves underneath, which were bulky and less easy to manoeuvre.

As the first woman vet to work in this lab, I didn't

expect the protective clothing given to me to fit the realms of the bespoke. While my eleven female colleagues situated throughout the labs in England, and comprising ten per cent of the veterinary workforce, had helped bring the organisation into the 1980s, and the Sex Discrimination Act 1975 had moved things forward, cultures and behaviours were changing with the enthusiasm of vegetarians for a full English breakfast.

Next on my list was a live pig submitted to investigate an arthritis problem in the herd it came from. Sometimes an affected animal had to be sacrificed so that we could examine fresh material to help us reach a diagnosis and I started by taking blood samples from the pig.

Like all species, pigs don't like having needles stuck into them and blood withdrawn. However, they are unlike other species in two respects: their veins are not palpable through the skin and they are able to emit, during both inhalation and exhalation, the noise of a McLaren F1 at top speed. A paediatrician once told me that taking blood samples from children shared the same problems.

Therefore, we were provided with ear-defenders for pig bleeding; headphones in reverse as they keep noise out rather than in. So far so mute. However, through some phenomenon of synaesthesia, I found I couldn't see very well when I wore the things designed for the expanse of a male skull and ears. But rather than spawn a stooshie or fuel a furore I sensed it was better to keep calm, carry on and, when no one was looking, take them off enabling me to find the vein right away.

I then examined the pig and observed it walk before euthanasing it. As Tom, the post-mortem room attendant hoisted the carcass onto the table for me, I saw Dick lurking in the doorway.

'Thought you'd a couple of days off, Dick,' I said.

He shrugged. 'Taking a quick break from rehearsals.'

Dick was a Morris dancer and long supporter of the Morris Ring, the traditionalist governing body which, unlike the Morris Federation which has allowed women dancers and musicians for a long time, denied until recent years the legitimacy of women members; similar to the Royal College of Veterinary Surgeons until 1922 when they admitted their first woman member.

Dick stood seraph-like in white knickerbockers, shirt and knee-length socks, bells around his legs, two red sashes forming a cross over his chest and a hat adorned with flowers.

'Expect you'll need a rest from hoppin' around to "*In an English Country Garden*",' Tom said in his East Anglian drawl.

Dick raised an eyebrow then said to me, 'How are you getting on with the problem at Linden?'

'This is the one they sent in,' I replied, pointing with my post-mortem knife to the pig on the table.

Dick nodded and craned his neck through the door.

I turned the pig over on its right side and began opening the abdomen, Dick staring like a child waiting for a Christmas present to be unwrapped.

'Stop,' he shouted. 'I'm coming in.'

I looked up, hands held above the carcase, while

I heard Dick's bells jingle and a rustling as he donned overalls, boots and an apron.

'There,' he said, pulling on Marigolds and walking into the post-mortem room, puffing a little and pointing to the pig's lower abdomen. 'Perfect. I'll take it.'

'What?' Tom and I asked in unison.

'The bladder,' Dick replied.

'What?' I repeated.

'It's full. I need a full one.'

'Why?'

'Empty ones don't work.'

I frowned.

Dick grasped the neck of the bladder with his left hand to prevent leaking of urine while he cut the organ out of the pig's abdomen. Holding it with the determined steadiness of an egg-and-spoon-race contestant, he walked to the sink to empty then refill it with formalin, a preservative.

Tom and I watched, still frowning and open-mouthed.

'It's for May Day celebrations tomorrow,' Dick explained to us, like a teacher to pupils of low IQ. 'I carry a pig's bladder on a stick and touch any maiden with it who wants a baby.'

'Oh,' I said. 'Does it work?'

'If they're not pregnant within a twelve month, the Morris men visit them.'

Tom shook his head. 'Dick's the Fool, Sheilagh,' he says.

'A fool?' I asked, resting my post-mortem knife on the table.

'The Morris Men's Fool. He'll whack the ones not dancing properly with the bladder.'

CLOTHES THAT COVER UP

As a house surgeon, I would on occasion wear scrubs. These loose-fitting cotton T-shirt tops and trousers are so much the embodiment of comfiness that they feel like pyjamas. While wearing them, I responded in a Pavlovian way by yearning for Ovaltine and bed, and standing in a packed waiting room was like one of these dreams when you find yourself naked in a crowd.

But some of the protective clothing I encountered wasn't quite so relaxing.

'Is this scuba gear really necessary?' asked John, my fellow veterinary investigation officer.

It was the later 1980s and the lab staff had met to discuss the new protective equipment provided for us when we were removing brains from cows suspected to have bovine spongiform encephalopathy, or BSE.

'We believe so, John,' answered Tony, our boss. 'I know that when we first heard of the disease a year or two ago, we assumed it was no more infectious to people than is scrapie ...'

'And scrapie brains, I would remind everyone, were once mashed up and fed to infants in some remote parts of Scotland without causing outbreaks of spongiform encephalopathies,' interjected John.

'Quite so,' said Tony, adjusting his half-rims. 'But scrapie appears to have jumped from sheep to cattle and so the possibility of a further jump to *Homo sapiens* cannot be ignored.'

We all nodded while gazing with a good degree of circumspection at the whole-face mask, hood, extraction hose and battery pack being demonstrated to us by Rory, the senior lab technician. We were instructed to wear these along with head-to-toe vinyl, thick rubber boots and stout rubber gloves while sawing open the invincible skulls of hapless 'mad cows' and it seemed quite an 'ask'.

We got used to it, of course, and whole brain removal was soon replaced with extraction of the brain stem through a natural whole in the base of the skull. But throughout the time we wore this aptly-dubbed scuba gear, we each probably lost our entire body weight in sweat and I for one emerged with the biceps of Schwarzenegger. Every cloud.

Disposable white boiler suits were the *sine qua non* of notifiable disease investigations. They were easily slipped on over clothes then off and squashed into a small ball for incineration at the end of a farm visit.

While dressed in these fetching onesies I'm not sure whether the startled response we got from both livestock keepers and livestock was down to the colour of the garments, the profiles we presented, both individually and as a group, or concern that their premises was being used for an episode of *Silent Witness*. But if it weren't for the disease-control properties of this attire we may well have replaced them with something better aligned to the typical human body. As everyone knows, white does anything but flatter the figure, making the question, 'does my bum look big in this?' superfluous and some of us had rather big tums in them, too. Nicky Alexanders, we were not.

'Look at this lot,' said Sarah, as she unloaded from her car several bags of equipment that she'd collected from a former quarantine kennel for dogs suspected to have rabies.

The bags included a canvas suit that was so rigid it stood up on its own, both jacket and trousers, in the absence of either human or mannequin.

'Try it on?' invited Sarah.

I shook my head, while attempting to manipulate the sleeves as uncompromising as Mussolini.

'Was a vet really expected to wear this while observing a potentially rabid dog?' I asked.

Sarah pulled a face and nodded. 'Better than getting rabies, though.'

While wishing to avoid any hint of ingratitude towards my former employers' diligence towards its staff, it may be fair to say that the protective clothing we were obliged to wear was similar to the organic apple: odd in shape, sometimes lacking in taste but always aimed at preserving good health.

12

Riding before I walk

On my back and in a ditch, I wiggle my left foot then my right. Spinal cord intact. My shirt feels damp, the smell of rotting vegetation inescapable, and I hear a motorbike whine on the A68. Sensory function effective. I look up into the nostrils of my horse, staring down at me with insouciance, and give thanks that I've survived another expulsion from her saddle.

If I said 'horse whisperer' maybe you'd think Robert Redford in tight jeans, cowboy boots and joined at the hip with the smokily simpering Kristin Scott Thomas.

Horse whispering or, less mysteriously, natural horsemanship took off in the late twentieth century although many practitioners who haven't enjoyed the renown of Monty Roberts, it's most famous exponent, insist that it's such an old philosophy it's become new again. This is probably true but they risk sounding as jealous of Monty as I am of Kristin.

In Europe, preparing horses for warfare influenced traditional methods of horse training, while the sometimes harsh methods employed by late nineteenth century cowboys in the American midwest to break in semi-feral mustangs came from the need to get them working on cattle ranches quickly. Punishing horses was as much part of the cowboys' training methods as Stetsons to their heads, pointy toes to their boots and premature ageing in their wives.

The natural horsemanship movement uses gentler methods learned from the cowboys of the Pacific north west. Horse trainers should nurture the horse-human relationship, the movement says, using training devised from observations of how horses communicate with each other.

But the part played by natural horsemanship in bringing change to horse owning in the UK was as fundamental as saddle soap to saddles. The reason lay in its Shire horse-size appeal to a population of inexperienced horse keepers which, at the turn of the twenty-first century, sprouted like mushrooms in horse poo.

'Move her between your heel and hand,' Sally barks as she watches me ride Scarlett around her arena.

I have no idea what she wants me to do.

Encouraged by horse-owning friends, and inspired by a book I read by Monty Roberts, I had begun riding in my fourth decade, relishing the challenge after many enjoyable years of keeping dogs. Scarlett was introduced to me as suitable for my novice-level riding skills but after a test ride with her I wondered whether we were as well matched as Miss Marple would be to Formula 1. But this thoroughbred chestnut mare was also lovely; athletically sleek and graceful within a Titian pulchritude. I looked at her the way Simba looked at Nala and bought her anyway.

In the months that followed my sense of being 'over-horsed' grew like ringworm. Whenever I asked Scarlett for canter within a few paces she would gallop. In itself, this was fine. Exhilarating even. The pupil-widening, palpitating potential lay in Scarlett's tendency to conclude with an abruptness that ejected me with greater force than a pilot from his burning Spitfire and gave me an uninvited acquaintance with the decayed depths of ditches.

It was Sally, a riding instructor and consummate rider, who first agreed to help improve my riding. She'd taken time out from eventing, a sport which originates in testing horses for the Cavalry, and I was beginning to feel she'd rather be back in her saddle than with a no-hoper newbie.

'What are you riding her in?' Sally asks, her apparent impatience rising with my confusion.

I wonder if she's referring to the make of my boots. She could surely see what else I was wearing.

'Sorry?' I ask, panting at the trot passed her, trying to keep my back straight and heels in line with my knees.

Sally glowers into her tweed and knee-high leather. 'What type of bit is in Scarlett's mouth?'

'Oh,' I reply, feeling stupid and annoyed that she hadn't asked that at first. 'It's a snaffle. Four inch,' I add as I pull the reins and bring Scarlett back to walk.

Sally nods, agrees it's the right one to use then suggests that's enough for today.

'You just need to spend time with her, Sheilagh. Enjoy hacking out and getting to know each other,' she advises as we walk back to her yard, then adds the incisive statement, 'there's nothing wrong with her.'

I tie Scarlett outside Sally's office then go in to pay. The walls are peppered with pictures of, what look like, her riding throughout her life, attended by supportive grown-ups. I point to one where a nursery-age child is lying stretched out along a pony's back, and smile.

Sally smiles, too. 'That's Smoky. One of my first ponies. I was recovering from chicken pox at the time.'

With the philanthropy of Saint Paul, Monty Roberts came to the UK in the late 1980s to bring the good news about kinder horse training methods. His first demonstration of 'join up' – creating a partnership with a horse – was to the Queen who agreed that his ideas had merit. Roberts's teachings led to interest in keeping horses in people hitherto unhorsey, but who felt drawn to this equine zeitgeist.

At the same time, in response to the prevailing agricultural crisis, farmers required other sources of income, and the love child of their union with aspiring horse owners was the Do-It-Yourself livery yard. In this win-win arrangement, horsekeepers paid farmers for use of a stable and grazing but cared for the horses themselves – mucking out, feeding, exercising, and turning out.

This worked like a well-oiled cart provided the horse owners had a degree of horsey knowledge. But the wheels came off with the less informed who, when they realised that horses are not big Labradors, had no one to ask what they should be doing.

Traditional instructors, born into horse keeping, pootling on ponies while still in nappies and competing in gymkhanas as soon as they could walk were sometimes inclined to an imperiousness and arcane language. They knew their Dutch gags from their girth straps and their cheek piece from their chaps, and became proficient with a bridle and hoof pick before a knife and fork, but seemed slightly reluctant to share their expertise with an equestrian hoi polloi.

On the other hand, the tone of natural horsemanship was egalitarian, accessible to us all; a Mahatma Gandhi to the Genghis Khan of classical horse keeping. The philosophies of Roberts and his peers were delivered in words everyone could understand, and enthusiasm was all you needed for the licence to spend your free time and disposable income on grooming, plaiting, shifting muck heaps and mastering the shoulder-in.

'What you need, Sheilagh, is a more holistic approach,' Maggie advises over the phone.

Holistic, I think. Crumbs.

After Sally's attempts to make a rider of me, I'd turned to Maggie, a livery yard owner also known for her natural horsemanship prowess.

'Not sure what you mean,' I say.

'You must learn to communicate with Scarlett in subtle ways, so you interact effectively.'

'Hmm.'

A day or two later I'm standing with Scarlett beside me in the middle of Maggie's round pen, bounded by high fencing. Maggie is outside, guiding us through 'join up'.

'Unclip the lead rope and send her away from you,' Maggie says.

'Um?'

'Use a dominant posture to make her trot around the pen.'

I look at Maggie, raising my eyebrows. She pushes a hand through her blonde highlights.

'Stand tall, move your arms away from your body. Stare at her.'

I do as Maggie says. Scarlett responds by lowering her head and nibbling grass.

'Look, I'll show you,' Maggie says, coming into the pen.

I step outside.

Maggie sends Scarlett trotting round the pen, one direction then the other, again and again before pointing to Scarlett's inner ear turned towards her. 'See that? It means she's ready to join up.'

Maggie drops her shoulders and head, then turns sideways to Scarlett who stops circling and walks towards her.

'She's an intelligent horse, Sheilagh,' Maggie concludes, 'nothing wrong with her.'

But this equine crusade had its dark side. In their multitude, natural horsemanship practitioners had their websites and online stores selling branded merchandise, glossy-paged pamphlets in low word to picture ratios and DVDs promising better riding in a few days and lessons in speaking 'horse'.

Debates as hot as bran mash followed over whether we should chase horses around a pen to bond with them. Join up doesn't help you accustom horses to unpleasant things like needles, the critics told us, and the 'natural' part of the name is misleading as nothing that we do with horses is natural – racing, cross-country and Sunday afternoon hacking are above the pay grade of animals designed to spend all day eating.

Eventually many trainers settled for a hybrid approach, selecting features of both traditional and horse whispering methods.

Then, around the time of the recession in 2008, the bubble of amateur horsekeeping turned into a helium balloon past its shelf life. Horses became recognised as an expensive pastime above Sky Sports in the list of 'things we might have to do without' and those whose hearts were never really in it sold their equines for half what they'd paid and moved on to hot yoga and the French bulldog.

I'm power walking. You have your shoulders back and down, head held as if suspended by a string, and place each foot with a rolling motion from heel to toe, elbows bent and arms moving forward and backwards with each pace. It's not high intensity stuff, but more dignified than a set of chest-to-floor burpees and dumbbell goblet squats.

I'm moving through the depth and silence of the woods at about fifteen minutes to the mile, enough to sweat and keep up with the whippet. My cadence is smooth. I'm meeting the requirements of this activity, basking in that blissful province between challenge and ease, and the ground, drenched with the dregs of melted snow, applauds my efforts with a repetitive squelch.

Oscar finds the wing of a long-dead pheasant and runs ahead, his trophy held high. He sees the horse before I do, drops his carrion and barks. I stop and call him. He hesitates for a moment then comes to me so I have him on his lead before the horse and rider meet us. It's Kathryn, a neighbour and trainer for National Hunt racing. She brings her horse to a halt with body movements only she and the horse know about.

'That's a nice one,' I say, nodding to her bay gelding, muscles as visible as ripples on water. 'Is he new?'

Kathryn nods. 'Ty, we call him. Got him at Doncaster last month. Has a full brother that won at Perth not so long ago.'

'Likely to have potential, then,' I say, then realise Kathryn would have bought him for no other reason.

Unlike my motive for buying Scarlett, the abandonment by reason of desire. When I'd confessed to Kathryn, she'd glanced down at her boots and offered to come with me next time I looked for a horse. But in the end it was my farrier, Charlie, persisting with the regular shoeing of this hot-blooded and beautiful mare, who had dared to suggest what only a good friend can.

'Are you sure this horse is right for you?' he asked with the careful candour he would use if I had body odour.

I handed Scarlett to Harriet, my strawberry-blonde

daughter, who rode her with a mortality-defying confidence and consecration of their enduring bond.

Returning to Ty I ask Kathryn, 'How's his training going?'

'So far so good. I've taken him hunting and we'll have a go at the point-to-point in a couple of weeks.'

Nodding, I rub Ty's forehead and stroke the warm velour of his muzzle.

'Well, must press on. Good to see you, Sheilagh.'

I watch Kathryn ride away, Ty's sweet spiciness on my hand enhancing that now familiar mix of envy and failure whenever I see someone as comfortable with a horse as I am with dogs.

I turn round, let Oscar off the lead then resume my walk, getting back into a rhythm. Oscar finds his pheasant bits. I build pace and, in time, think about the origins of a horse's unique aroma, why it is that on the darkest and dankest of bankings snowdrops proliferate so invincibly, and how on earth you teach a dog to stop rolling in fox poo.

13

Dad

'The influence of each human being on others in this life is a kind of immortality.'

JOHN QUINCY ADAMS

If writing a biography is about trying to make sense of things, composing biographical details of one's parents should serve this end well.

Using photographs, my memories, others' recollections and my father's obituaries that I kept, still with the entire newspapers published in the mid October days following his death in 1983, I have described from an adult perspective how I remember my father and with a better appreciation than I had during his lifetime of the impacts of trauma and privation.

Robert Nisbet was an ordinary man who led in the twentieth century a generally unremarkable life not dissimilar to many of his peers: he fought in the Second

World War, returned to study at university, married and had three children. And although he would have been upset to think that a story about his life proposed that he was in any way exceptional, I believe he may have approved of an account describing the ways in which he showed how ordinary people may live their lives to the full, make the best of everything offered to them and, as much as possible, impact on the lives of others in a positive, rewarding way.

Sophocles said, 'One must wait until the evening to know how splendid the day has been' and it follows that so often we do not fully appreciate the extent of a person's goodness until after their death. Although my father's legacy has become evident to me only as I have become the age at which he died, however late, it is worthy of documenting.

My father was born on 30 June 1920 to Peter Nisbet and his second wife, Catherine. I'm not sure why I didn't know about his two half sisters until after my father died. Helen and Catherine, children of Peter and his first wife who had died of TB, lived with my father's family for some time and so I would expect to have heard something about them.

Peter died in 1925, also of TB, leaving my grandmother to bring up my father, Maud his younger sister and his two elder half-sisters. My grandmother, known as Katie, was given a pension of the equivalent of 80p per week so, although they didn't starve, the family lived frugally. Sometime later, Katie's elder sister, Annie, also widowed and with three daughters, moved in with them, allowing them to pool their resources and find work to supplement their widows' pensions. Although it must have been a crowded house, the cheerfulness and sanguine nature of my father and Auntie Maud, suggest that it had been a loving and supportive upbringing as far as resources had allowed. Annie was, however, a redoubtable figure, who appeared to have taken her younger sister in hand, leading the combined families and ensuring strict discipline.

It was Annie, I am told, who insisted that my father leave school at 14 years to begin to contribute to the family income, although he expressed a desire to stay on at school and further his education. So, it was with some regret that he accepted his new place in the family as a provider. His first job as a telegram boy ended when he joined the Territorial Army in 1938 because he wanted to learn to drive. With the outbreak of the second world war in 1939, he was mobilised with the 1st Lothians and Border Yeomanry (LBY) to France.

In April 1940, my father and the rest of the LBY were transferred to the 51st (Highland) Division, which continued to fight while the rest of the British Expeditionary Force was evacuated from Dunkirk. The 51st then attempted to recapture Abbeville but after a German counter-attack, they retreated to St Valéry en Caux hoping that the Royal Navy and a few small ships would help them escape. However, due to thick fog and Stuka dive bombing of the beaches, this wasn't possible. My mother recalls my father telling her that he and others had hid in caves along the beaches when they saw that men trying to reach the waiting ships were killed. When the French surrendered, the 51st was left to fight on its own before they, too, were surrendered on 12 June 1940 by Major General Fortune to General Rommel.

What followed for my father, and the 10,000 or so other British troops taken prisoner on that day, has been scarcely documented, and my mother, in whom my father confided, has told me most of what I know. The forced march through Belgium into Germany in 1940, during which Dad spent his 20th birthday, involved sleeping in fields and with very little to eat, and was followed by five years of captivity in the German Stalags. The image of the Stalags portrayed in Hogan's heroes, the American TV sitcom of the late 1960s and 1970s set in the fictional Stalag 13, provided no insight into the scarce food allowance, disease and violent treatment from guards that the Prisoners of War suffered. My father was in Nazi Stalag XXb near Marienburg in, what was then, West Prussia. The bunk beds were several high in cramped rooms but with plenty of rats. The POWs were infested with lice and the toilet consisted of a trench with a tree trunk across it; unsurprisingly, diarrhoea was common.

Prisoners of my father's rank were required to work and consequently, he was sent to a sugar beet factory and then to a farm in Poland. When I worked as a student on a dairy farm, I remember a conversation with Dad when, drawing on his war time work, he commented how cows in late pregnancy can have a particular docility and glow; exactly my observations.

In their fifth winter of captivity in 1945, the POWs were marched away from the Russian army to Holland, after which they were liberated, and returned home. In 1940, the men had been relatively fit but after five years of hard work on a poor diet, the heavy snow falls and freezing conditions of this winter along with the continuing privations were fatal to many. Witnessing the death of a number of his fellow POWs left my father humbled and grateful throughout the rest of his, albeit short, life that he had survived.

Although he shared with my mother some of what happened to him, my father rarely spoke to us, his children, of his time in captivity other than an occasional remark about the moments that had brought him some respite; like getting to know the ordinary people in the places where he worked and learning their language and culture, which he clearly came to hold in high regard. He told us about the intermittent Red Cross parcels in which each POW was given a small bar of chocolate, five cigarettes and a jar of blackcurrant purée. This was sour, unpalatable stuff that many of the POWs refused to eat, but my father considered it would do him good and he found that a few of his smoker friends were only too willing to swap their jar for one of his cigarettes. And my sister Val reminded me recently of a particularly funny story that Dad told us about the times when he and his fellow POWs, while learning German, practised on the Stalag guards, young men as they were away from their homes and families. The German for 'what time is it' is 'wie spät ist es' which, when spoken quickly sounds a bit like 'fish paste'. It amused Dad and his friends when a guard, on seeing them point to the back of their wrist and name this foodstuff, would reply with the time.

I do not recall my father ever complaining nor seeking sympathy for the hardships he sustained during the war. Indeed, he appeared to enjoy watching Hogan's Heroes with us and laughing at the bumbling Commandant Klink and his equally incompetent Sergeant Schultz. Dad also pointed out that were it not for the war, he would not have had the educational opportunities offered to him. Not only did he learn to drive but with the offer made to war veterans to study at Edinburgh University, he pulled himself out of early- to mid-twentieth century poverty to gain a master's degree in 1950 and become a primary school teacher. This, with my mother's help, enabled him to provide for my sister Val, brother Robin and me a more comfortable upbringing than my grandmother had been able to offer him.

After his first appointment at Bonington Primary School in Leith, he taught at Auchterarder, Perthshire before becoming headteacher of Portmoak Primary School in Kinrosshire. He then became head of the primary school in Muckhart before moving to become headteacher at Comrie Primary School. He died in that post. At his funeral, parents and pupils of many years back joined the huge congregation in Comrie, Perthshire.

Dad approached every responsibility he took with the dedication, energy and enthusiasm for which he was widely known while remaining self-effacing, modest and humble. Being praised made him uncomfortable, he hated recognition and he always went the extra mile.

After school hours, in his own time, he trained his school football team and took pride in their achievements at matches throughout Perthshire. I recall our family Mini Traveller accommodating many of his school football team, there being no other way of making sure the boys could take part in matches with other schools. The range of his activities for the school and the wider communities was breath-taking: he did all the school administration without secretarial assistance and while teaching his own senior class; he was a member of the Comrie Dramatic Society, an elder of the church and took part in the school's Parent Teacher Association where his measured suggestions and guidance were much appreciated. The trust he placed in his staff engendered team work and decision-making that would have been the envy of many senior corporate executives.

Dad was widely known for his quiet kindliness, compassion and patience, and pupils and their parents were very fond of him. He held the conviction that a good education would open doors and facilitate a better life, and to this end his commitment to the children in his care left their parents feeling privileged that their offspring attended his school.

Foremost, my father was devoted to us and our mother. He even named a favourite picnic place 'Valshebob' after us. I can think of nothing he did for himself, other than sitting in an armchair watching football with a cup of tea in the few minutes following our weekly swimming trip to Perth and before leading the Saturday night children's badminton club. He appeared to reject the concept of 'me time'.

I am in awe of the courage and determination he showed to take the five of us away for camping holidays in a Mini Traveller with an engine capacity of less than one litre, a tent, cooker, tins of stew, sleeping bags, clothes and the inflatable canoe around Europe. Today, I drive a car of similar size and tremble when I take it on the M6 and with nothing like the cargo. But danger is a relative and subjective concept. After his experience twenty five years or so before these holidays as a Prisoner of War, my father was probably grateful to be free, fed, watered, housed, clothed and with people he loved. After crouching in a shelter, boots falling apart, emaciated with dysentery and infested with lice, praying that the allied bombers saw the red cross sign on the roof and that their aim was good, a three-thousand-mile adventure with his wife and three young children in a tiny car would have been like a trip to the local Tesco.

It would be the summer holiday of 1965 or thereabouts when Val, Robin and I returned from a play park on a camp site where we were staying near to a fast-flowing stretch of the Rhine River to see a man with only one arm shouting in German and pointing across the river with his hand. Dad rushed out of our tent, followed by Mum.

'Someone's drowning,' Dad said, looking where the man was pointing.

As we watched Dad sprint down the river bank, a few people had gathered at the edge of the water, looking at a child bobbing up and down and being pushed along with the strong current. Mum stood, eyes wide and mouth open, staring at my father. When he was a good distance downstream from the child in the water, Dad stopped and dived in. It seemed ages before we saw him resurface and then, half swimming, half taken along by the current, he moved across the river to meet the child, whom I could then see was a boy. Dad grabbed him and working with the strong current, swam down stream, gradually in towards the bank, still holding the boy. Later, he was able to grasp something on the banking – I can't remember what. We all ran down to them. My father pushed the boy out of the water then got out himself. He was dressed in his shorts, socks, old shirt. Still with his sandals on.

We left the following day, heading for Switzerland, the next leg of our journey in Europe. I don't remember giving the incident much further thought but now, as well as admiring Dad's enormous courage and selflessness, I feel shocked at the thought of what might have happened; of what he risked in diving into a fast-flowing river to save a stranger's life. The owner of the German camping site gave Dad a bottle of wine and thousands of miles later when we got home, there was a letter waiting from the boy's father enclosing a photograph. My mother still has it – a blond eight-year-old standing in a garden with roses, a picture that would not have been were it not for my Dad.

By the next year, my Dad had upgraded from the Mini traveller to a Morris 1100. He'd wanted another Mini on account of the frugal running costs but my brother, sister and I were all getting bigger and the lack of space on long journeys was causing as much tension as the Harlem race riots.

'Whose turn is it to sit in the middle?' was the oft repeated question whenever we embarked on a long journey and, I feel sure, was one of the reasons both my brother and sister limited their own families to two. I, on the other hand, went on to have five children, but that's another story.

Our anticipation of a more comfortable journey over the 2000 kilometres to our camping site in the South West of France was dashed when my sister's friend, Ann, joined us. Our parents probably thought that four kids would make for more harmony than three, and indeed it did, but we were back to where we were with lack of space. Dad's determined philosophy to make the best of everything saw him make a seat across the hand brake for my brother to perch between the two front seats while Val, Ann and I rolled about, seatbeltless yet safe, in the back.

We travelled overnight from Perthshire to Dover, a journey that left us tired and grumpy and my Dad exhausted. We stopped in Calais for a couple of nights. Maybe it was the additional responsibility of someone else's child or maybe he was just especially worn out that year, but Dad told us over our tinned stew and boiled potatoes that evening that we might spend the whole holiday there.

'What?' I said, 'and not go to Socoa?

'Yes,' Dad replied, 'why not. It's nice in this camp site. The beach is nearby and it would save us a lot of travelling.'

'But we like Socoa,' we all wailed.

Dad nodded.

The next afternoon, we were swimming in the Channel when we noticed that a shoal of jelly fish had joined us. The colours filled the UV spectrum and we wondered in awe at their delicate tendrils as they drifted over our tummies in the shallow water. It was when I got dried and put on a T shirt that I felt my skin stinging and soon it reached the crescendo of a million wasps landing on me at once. I noticed Ann frowning and rubbing her arms and soon we were all complaining of widespread itching, burning skin.

We tried calamine lotion, cold water, a long walk to take our minds off it, even the expensive French ice creams, while I heard my Dad mutter to my Mum something along the lines of a rush back to Dover and an NHS hospital. By the next day, the stinging had gone along with Dad's desire to stay in Calais, so we set off for the south-west along France's pre-motorway routes.

The 1100 was well loaded with the paraphernalia required for a camping holiday for six – big tent, poles, gas cooker, sleeping bags, food, besides the said six people – so my Dad reduced the strain on the suspension by rarely putting more than a couple of gallons of petrol in the tank at one time.

'Why are we stopping here?' Robin asked from his inter-seat perch.

Val, Ann and I looked up from our books as Dad pulled the car in to the right side of the road. The engine died. Cars behind gave a two-fingered peep before overtaking and after he got out the car, Dad gave them an apologetic wave and shrugged his shoulders. We had run out of petrol. Again. Just like we had outside Amiens.

Mum steered as the rest of us pushed until another driver stopped. His car had a 'D' beside the number plate and Dad was delighted to practice his wartime-learned German. They chatted away, laughing, shaking their heads, then the man got into his car and drove off.

'That nice man is going to get some petrol for us.' Dad brought us up to speed. 'He won't be long.'

It took four days through Biaritz, Bayonne then St Jean de Luz, but we got to Socoa, enjoyed our camping holiday fuelled with Woolies tinned mince, local potatoes and the enormous French peaches then travelled all the way back to Perthshire. And only now do I appreciate what Dad achieved in doing so, for us, his family. Only now, when I consider these things deep in my memory do I realise Dad's understanding and articulation of the diverse expressions of love.

'Why don't you apply for medicine,' he asked me about ten years later while I was completing the university entrance forms on the dining table, 'you've got the grades for that.'

I resisted all parental suggestions then simply on account of their provenance.

'Dad,' I replied as if speaking to an idiot, 'I've got the grades required for veterinary medicine.'

There are times when I look back on my younger versions and not like what I see. It was a time when other stuff was going on in my life that he didn't understand and I'm not sure I do now. So he wrote me a letter and put it on my bed. He admires me and berates me and asks me to be more tolerant. I wrote back telling him what I couldn't say to him; that I loved him. I kept his letter and each time I read it I take away a new message, a new slant on something, another way of thinking.

If not exceptional, what was notable about my father was that, without a hint of ostentatiousness, he had a way of being, probably rooted in his religious faith, that could be summed up simply as love. His espousal of kindness and tolerance, of being nice, influenced everything he did and said. And he was proof of how far a positive attitude, cheerfulness and determination can offset straightened circumstances. He avoided boastfulness and advised that it was acceptable to be a success as long as you did so without showing off. Mistrusting commercial gain, he maintained that academic success was a far more worthy attainment, while self-reliance and accepting responsibility for one's fate were not obligations to him but empowering philosophies. And he represented all that was gentle in my life.

The shock and grief of losing him are with me still, as raw and real as on the morning he died. They sneak up when I'm going about life; as when I free the mirror of steam after my morning shower, I see Dad demisting the car windscreen with the back of his left hand, his short muscular fingers with nails trimmed well down, his gold signet ring making the glass squawk. I hear his deep inhalation and tutting when I crunch my gearbox or hit potholes and remember his instruction to treat the gear lever like an egg. And every time I see someone push their glasses back on the bridge of their nose, I see my Dad achieve the same effect with a brief wrinkle of his nose.

My father's death at the age of 63 was sudden and cruel. Bewildering. At the time, Val was pregnant with the first of his nine grandchildren whose lives he would have enriched beyond measure. But the legacies of this ordinary and quietly inspirational man are very much alive.

14

ON VOLUNTEERING

Detergent-adorned darkness infuses the early morning hospital lobby. The hospital cleaning staff sit in the bench seats nearest to the hospital café and give me a loud glance as the big shutter door rolls up like a measuring tape.

'They were heading for it. Made some daft decisions,' says Mandy, the cleaner with peroxide spikes and a snake tattoo on her left wrist.

'Shame about the thirty-eight out of a job now. Not fair on them.'

The others nod at Malcolm's comment. He looks at his tummy and I think of the crisps and Kit Kats I've sold him when he comes to empty our bins and remove the coffee grounds for composting.

This is my first volunteering shift for the café when I must open it up on my own, and I want to get it right. I start to pack away yesterday's papers – one or two Daily Express's and Daily Mails and a good few Daily Telegraphs and Heralds – and remember about noting the numbers of each on the returns list. Then I tie them into a bundle. On with the unpacking of today's papers.

'Have you got a Guardian?' I hear and look up to see a drip stand with a tube attached to a spindle-shaped arm.

'The café doesn't open till eight,' I advise the owner of the arm, 'but if you've got the right change and you promise not to tell my boss … ,' I add with a smile.

The man smiles back and counts out the money, placing it by the till for me to put in later, while I find his paper. His slippers sweep the vinyl floor as he turns back to the ward, pushing his drip stand with the attached arm and holding his paper in the other, and I feel that warm glow from helping someone's day get off to a better start, even though I've curved a rule.

'Nairns might take some of them on,' asserts Mandy, not dropping the main theme in yesterday's local rag of the building firm going into receivership.

Next, filling some shelves. Red top papers on the top shelves, broad sheets on the lowest ones. Then the bottles in the chiller – Ribena, Coke, Lucozade, Irn bru, Red Bull – and big bags of sweets and chocolate bars on opposite shelves. More for a kids' party than health-promoting patients' fare and I smile at the contrariness.

'Here's a pound. I'll take a can now, if you don't mind.'

As brassy as her spikes is Mandy – she knows the tills aren't ready yet. I nod and put the coin beside the Guardian money and watch her swagger away, ripping off the ring pull on her full-fat coke.

Just a few months earlier, I had sat down with Simon, the manager for the volunteer-run café at my local hospital.

'So, Sheilagh, we need to put down your reasons for wanting to join us,' he said.

We were going through my application form while he sipped a large hot chocolate and munched McCoys Flame Grill.

I looked for inspiration in Simon's round face. I recognised him as, a few kilos ago, a local high school's scrum-half as well as its pipe band leader. This afternoon, his supine attitude was contradicted in nails bitten to the quick and in his forehead beaded with perspiration like rain on glass. His light grey polo shirt suggested he wasn't into the culture of a separate white wash.

I'd heard that people volunteer for many reasons including keeping active, feeling connected and, at a time when their own social roles have changed, making use of their expertise to improve others' lives.

But I didn't know all this when, at the age of 58 and a half years, I left my job as a vet and started to draw down my pension. Note that I don't say 'retired'. I avoid the 'r' word because it makes me feel the age my birth certificate implies and suggests I spend my days tending flower beds and playing bingo. A friend, Alan, advised me to give myself two months to reflect before my next move.

It wasn't long before time, like rain in Scotland, never seemed to run out. I took to long walks in the woods with my dog, dawdling while trying to learn the art of mindfulness, as slippery as Cantonese, and I found that thinking about something absorbing was more restful;

like the advantages in losing social status, how many solar systems there are, why the best parts of porridge are those that stick to the bottom of the pan and whether that's a metaphor for something more profound. However, I was bored and needed to recover some sense of self-worth.

But all that wouldn't fit in the four by fourteen centimetre box on the application form and besides, I didn't want to share it with a fresh-faced man probably no older than my youngest child.

'We could put that you want to make friends,' Simon suggested, glancing at a device around his wrist, a nifty thing with a black face, no numbers, no hands.

I nodded, then remembered another reason I'd considered. 'Maybe learn new skills, too?'

When looking for a volunteering opportunity, I'd wondered around a local shop run by one of the charities for a life-limiting disease. I noted that its customers, rather than patched and impoverished, were fragrant and fulsome, and on the rails Florence and Fred rubbed its musty lapels into the elegant brocade of Jaeger. There were glass-fronted cabinets inside which stylish arrays of shoes, belts and hats helped enliven the pre-loved goods although their combined age weighed down the ambience like dark green foliage and a ticking grandfather clock in a Victorian Parlour. However, I decided not to volunteer there not because of any of the foregoing but because there appeared to be more volunteers than customers. The hospital café, on the other hand, whenever I had visited for various appointments over the years, had always seemed understaffed.

The next day, I began training to serve behind the café tills. The first delight of my new role was having a reason to wear something other than blue jeans and wellies, my usual dog-walking attire. So, in my black Pepes and Fly of London tan boots, things I'd forgotten I'd had, I went through the main entrance of the hospital, where the automatic doors whoosh with the frequency of a hyperventilating dragon. Opposite the gents, there was an elderly lady at the hospital's welcome desk shivering. I introduced myself.

'Oh, you're going to help in the café? That's nice. I'm Eleanor. If you go through these doors,' she said pointing with a tree-root hand on the end of a slender arm to the other end of the café, 'you'll find Simon.'

I walked through the café seating area with small round tables and wooden seats. Cacophonous groups of nurses wearing powder blue scrubs had gathered for a coffee and slice of Madeira and elderly couples sat opposite one another, sipping from paper cups in silence. I could see a father alone with his pink-enrobed newborn, her size in indirect proportion to the decibels she emitted and there was what appeared to be an entire family enjoying an opportunity for a get-together. Perhaps they were waiting for someone in A&E, or just liked the aura of the café but, whatever, they were laughing like hyenas, swapping stories and quaffing hot drinks and chocolate fudge.

My till training lasted five minutes and, once fitted out with a polo shirt with twice the white and half the cloth of Simon's, I took my place alongside a tiny lady with a blue badge saying 'volunteer' pinned to her shirt. We introduced ourselves.

'How long have you been volunteering, Patricia?' I asked, as she wiped the minute stainless steel sink, refilled the hot chocolate machine, replenished stocks of tea bags, cartons of soup and sugar sachets and dusted the acrylic surfaces around both tills before tidying up the paper cups. Watching her was more tiring than climbing Ben Vorlich.

'Oh, well, let's see,' she considered my question, in an alternate frowning and raising of her grey eyebrows. She glanced up at the chrome bean-to-cup coffee machine behind us. 'You're nice and tall. Can you put more beans in the tank at the top, please?'

I obliged as she adjusted her silver-rimmed glasses, smoothed her navy apron then washed her hands.

'About twenty five years. Since my children grew up and left home.'

'Goodness,' I said. 'You must enjoy it.'

She nodded. 'It's changed, though. All we used to offer were instant coffee and tea and we made the sandwiches ourselves. None of that,' she said turning towards the chiller cabinets with rows of pre-packed BLT, chicken pesto, tuna and sweetcorn, and an odd looking wrap with chickpeas poking through the cut surface.

'You'll have helped so many people who've used the hospital,' I added.

She shrugged. 'I've got as much out of it. Still find these things difficult, though.'

She pointed to the computerised till with the touch screen in front of her.

It wasn't long before I'd completed numerous shifts, and met all the common problems and quirks; like soup is charged using the till's 'tea' icon. Obviously. And we're not permitted to sell paracetamol, which often provokes intimations of irony.

I was relishing the fast-paced atmosphere. 'Hell hath no fury like a bored Sheilagh' a friend once remarked and I would certainly agree with Voltaire when he observed that work is the father of pleasure. Other volunteers began to turn to me for help, ladies like Patricia who, under their belts and within their aprons, had decades of service for the charity but for whom twenty first century IT systems were as palatable as wasabi.

I met Lydia during my first shift on a Monday morning. Her usual volunteer partner was, in Lydia's words, 'partying around South Africa' and catching up with some of her great-grandchildren.

'You'll know my cousin then, Richard White,' she said when I told her where I lived. 'We grew up together.' She shook her head. 'Bit of a character.'

'Yes,' I smiled at her and studied her face before adding, 'tricky dicky of Denston.'

'Goodness, I've heard him referred to as much worse than that.'

In spite of the years between us, I came to sense a kindred spirit in this well-spoken lady with a gleam that left her seventy-five-year-old eyes only when the queue reached double figures or the hot chocolate machine's output resembled the Tay in full spate.

A few joint shifts later, she confided that her husband had passed away the previous year and it was volunteering that helped her emerge from the dark times that followed.

'Made me get out again,' she said, 'and make friends. I enjoy being busy, too.'

Perhaps it was a squeamishness that stopped me from adding that the motive that kept me offering my time, doing extra shifts and being as flexible as Darcey Bussell was the extent to which I was helping myself, gaining an intangible reward of feeling good, in helping others.

Things are going fine with my first solo opening up of the café. Next, I count a £100 float into each of the two tills and fire them up ready for use, keeping an eye on the clock. Ten minutes before opening. Time to check the coffee machine is producing the best coffee for at least five miles. I open a bag of dark roasted beans and pour them into the reservoir and before I put the bag in the recycle bin, I take a spiriting sniff inside it, long and deep. Next, I take a shot glass and place it under the nozzle then press the single espresso button. There's a promising grinding, a siphoning and then a thick, dark, brown brew trickles into the glass, forming a beige foam on the surface. Perfect. The astringent bouquet, at 0752 hours and having left my house two hours earlier with an oatcake and Babybel cheese to sustain me, has the impact on my olfactory system of 40% ABV alcohol, and I bring it closer to my nose for a further fix before downing it in one. Utter blessedness. What more divine a spin-off could volunteering give.

I fill the milk jug and place it near the trolley of sugars and stirrers just as Edith, one of our diminutive septuagenarian volunteers, walks through the hospital entrance. I bid her good morning.

'Morning, Sheilagh,' she replies as she takes off her coat, hangs it up, puts on her navy apron then starts to loosen stacks of latte cups, as the A&E staff walk towards us.

I recognise the lady with the stethoscope scarf who always has a double espresso, so grab a tiny cup as she approaches. She sees it in my hand and nods. I press the icon to deliver the brunette nectar.

'Good morning,' I greet her, '£1.80 please.'

She smiles and hands me the cash. Then I notice Edith staring at her till.

'This funny screen won't go away,' she says.

She removes her reading glasses, gives them a quick clean and puts them back on before running her hands through her well coiffured white hair. The queue in front of us is reaching the hospital entrance.

I start making my next customer's small cappuccino then while the steamed milk and coffee shot pour into the cup, I look at Edith's screen. It has indeed gone funny. I hand over the hot drink, take the man's £2.00, then close my till.

'Okay,' I say, taking account of the waiting customers, 'you take my till, Edith. I'll shut down and reboot yours while I make the hot drinks.'

Edith and I work like a well-oiled machine and I'm enjoying my role as her Barista when a woman cuts across the queue and stands, rubbing red eyes and wet cheeks, in front of the counter.

'I can't find my husband,' she wails, 'been w...w... waiting for ages,' sniff, gulp, 'said he'd bring the car round to pick me up at the entrance,' more sniffing and eye rubbing, 'hasn't come b…b…back. Aaaargh.'

We all stare at each other. Edith's till confirms new life with a ping.

After a few seconds, I say, 'Edith, would you take the lady over to reception and ask them to look through the car parks for her husband.'

Edith, in her element, swings into action with consummate ease.

'Come with me, we'll find him. Don't worry. Look, here's a tissue,' she says to the abandoned wife, offering her a piece of kitchen towel from behind the counter.

For the nth time this morning I turn to replenish the gluttonous milk tank supplying the coffee machine.

'Large cappuccino.' I hear from behind me.

I look round to the largest, reddest nose I've ever seen from which escape alcohol fumes that, if passive drinking exists, will be sufficient to give me liver cirrhosis.

'Certainly. With chocolate sprinkles?' I smile as I grab a 15oz cup and press the top right button of the machine.

'Nah, I'm sound.'

I've come to learn many phrases used in the place of 'No, thank you': a shake of the head accompanied by 'I'm good'; 'I'm fine, thanks'; 'spoiling me, eh?'; 'trying to bankrupt me?'; 'you've been on a sales course,' wink, wink.

So I get the gist of this one and as I hand the customer his sprinkle-less frothy coffee, I look into a face that is as sound as a three-legged horse: above his red nose, eyes with yellowed whites protrude from a backdrop of greenish skin suggesting advanced jaundice.

Although, in volunteering it hadn't occurred to me that I might hone my diagnostic skills, it is an interesting spin off to see the array of clinical issues presented in our customers. This also helps me empathise with them, and offer additional assistance with diplomacy and respect. However, one man I couldn't help had symptoms suggesting Parkinson's disease and whose shaking hands repeatedly entered the wrong PIN number when he tried to pay by card. Fortunately, he had just enough cash on him.

The queue is beginning to ease off, and I'm topping up the coffee bean reservoir when Edith comes back.

'We found him,' she says, wiping down the surfaces and filling up the milk tank while stacking cup lids, 'the lost husband. Sitting in the top car park reading the sport pages of the Telegraph.'

The intricacies of IT may have escaped her but she cannot be bettered when it comes to helping solve other people's problems

Of course there are some disadvantages in working for nothing and the one I've experienced, the one that's really self-inflicted, is over-commitment. Doing too much. Not feeling able to say no when asked to do further shifts because if I decline, the café might have to close for the evening. Weekend and evening shifts are hard to fill as these times often clash with volunteers' family commitments but, nonetheless, I've had to learn to set limits to the time I offer and to become more resourceful with my suggestions as to how else the café can cover vacant shifts.

Not everyone can afford to work for nothing, too, and I expect this is why most of the volunteers I know are either of pension or school age; the majority of adults who volunteer in the United Kingdom are in the 65-80-year-old age group, although attempts are being made to involve larger numbers of young people by offering rewards such as a cinema ticket for a period of voluntary work. So, although it implies elements of selfishness, this arrangement encourages altruism in younger people. However, what many young people need as much as money and gifts is experience with people, assuming responsibility and using their initiative, as well as the reference to their voluntary work on their CVs. I know a recruiter who, when sifting through multiple applications from graduates all equally and highly qualified, looks for evidence of something extra like voluntary work to decide whom to invite for interview.

The morning shift is going well and my till is nicely full of ten and twenty pound notes as well as forests of card receipts, reflecting how busy we are. Katie and Megan, two of the café's employed assistants, join us and start to tidy and fill shelves, while I continue to serve, Edith has a break and Simon reviews stock levels in between doing the banking in the shop's office and answering the phone.

The average age of the assistants is less than half mine and little more than one third of most of the volunteers' I work alongside. I enjoy the atmosphere the assistants bring to the café but need an urban dictionary to gain some understanding of their language.

'I was fraped at the weekend,' Katie says as she man-handles thirteen kilos worth of bottled water between shelf and store trolley as if it were a box of Kleenex. Takes some courage to frape her, I think, even by the virtual means of Facebook.

'That's what you get for adding that douch-bag Tom,' advises Megan, her work 'bestie', with a swish of auburn hair plaited into a fishtail while lining up Mars Bars in two neat rows.

Jeff, a septuagenarian volunteer of small stature but with the wiriness and tensile strength of the Forth Bridge, teeth like fence posts and who used to drive lorries up and down the M6 with a ferocity to match Boudicca, walks into the shop and starts unloading bottles of soft drinks onto the shelves. Besides the hard labour, he brings a unique angle to team discussions, and I decide to tell them about the naming of my sons' old Land Rover.

'I wanted to call it "Hector" but Andrew and Hamish prefer "Imogen". Why do men regard engines as female?' I ask the team while they begin sorting through a box of bananas and filling little punnets with green and black grapes.

'My car isn't female,' objects Simon as he helps Katie separate some green, juicy globes from their stalks. 'He's called Rupert and I call my bagpipes Bertie.'

I'd heard that Simon and Bertie had travelled the world together for pipe band competitions and been through many trials like being held up in airports while they body searched Bertie for white powders with eye-watering street value.

Katie nods. She has washers in her ear lobes. You can see through the holes and hear a faint whistle whenever she moves her head. 'Yes, I'm with Simon on this. I've had male cars and female cars. It all depends on their personalities.'

Jeff adds his views. 'All the Scanias I had were female. Broke down at the worst times. Fickle, blinking things.'

'I think it has naval roots,' steps in Malcolm, who arrives to empty our bins for us. 'Sailors' wives looked after them on land so the ships who took care of them at sea had to be female, too.'

Katie rolls her eyes and glances at Jeff. 'Hmm. Proves men can't look after themselves.'

'Why is it, then?' Megan asks, returning to my original question.

'I'm not sure,' I say, while taking a fresh bin liner from Malcolm and fitting it into the dark green bin, 'but there was a Rear Admiral Foley of the US Navy, who stated that a ship had to be female because she has a gang of men around her, she requires a lot of paint to keep her good looking, it's not her initial cost that is troublesome but her upkeep and it takes an experienced man to handle her correctly.'

Katie crushes the banana in her hand, Simon and Malcolm wince, and Jeff clutches his sides then wipes tears from his eyes.

I decide the cubby holes under the counter need tidying up, then greet a wheezing gentleman walking towards the counter.

'Have you got a cup of tea?' he rasps then explodes with a rapid succession of loud, crippling coughs.

I watch as his face turns red then deep red then an alarming purplish red and I'm relieved when the coughing stops and he sucks in sufficient air to restore his face colour to less worrying hues.

'Yes, of course,' I reply, 'are you okay?'

He nods, leaning on the counter and looking at the floor while his chest expands and contracts. I put a tea bag in a cardboard cup, fill it with boiling water from the urn, fit a lid and as I turn round to put it on the counter, the man begins to sway.

'Wait a minute,' I say, 'let me get you a chair.'

'There's a wheelchair just there,' a lady behind him in the queue steps in to help. 'I'll get it.'

She puts her purchases on the counter then rushes towards the wheelchair while the man who was behind her in the queue holds the swaying gentleman.

'It's okay,' he reassures him, 'here's a chair for you.'

I walk from behind the counter and the three of us guide him into the wheelchair. I try not to cough myself at the paralysing smell of cigarette smoke he radiates.

The queue is getting bigger now.

'I'll take him through to A&E,' the lady says to me, nodding towards the queue, 'let you get on.'

While I resume serving I reflect on how incidents like this can bring out the best in people, how bystanders think nothing of stopping their busy days to offer kindness and selflessness.

Simon returns to the shop from the office with a tray of fivers and coins from the banking as the man is wheeled towards A&E.

'That's old Jim,' Simon says to me, 'I see him in town quite a bit.'

'I hope he's okay,' I say as Simon changes the notes and coins in his tray for ten and twenty pound notes in my till.

Simon nods.

Volunteering, doing something unpaid that benefits the community, is thought to have evolved in this country in the twelfth century from the volunteer hospitals, while the cottage hospitals began around the mid-nineteenth century, run by doctors with an income from their private practices. In 1948, Bevan's NHS Acts allowed for the public funding of hospitals and hospital staff, and that now, in the twenty-first century, many NHS hospitals rely on their large cadre of volunteers to support the employed staff, is not without some irony.

Volunteers work for many other organisations including the police, charities and libraries, and rather than replacing salaried staff, the volunteers work alongside and complement the paid staff's work.

Lady Stella Reading, who founded the Women's Voluntary Service in 1938 to help civilians during and after air raids and to organise the evacuation and billeting of children commented that many people considered volunteers to be a means to an end, as free labour. But voluntary service, she said, was not like that. Instead, it was the gift of a kind person of their skills, their energies and their time. Now known as the Royal Voluntary Service, the charity has about 35,000 volunteers.

Edith returns from her break, so I take the chance to visit the loo. As I'm washing my hands, I see above the sink a poster advertising the hospital canteen's hot meals, snacks and range of hot and cold drinks, all pictured in bright, shiny colours and right next to it another poster encouraging you to submit a poo sample for bowel cancer screening. The relationship is as obvious as the juxtaposition is unappetising.

As I leave the cubicle, I see a poster on the door with different shades of green, advising you to check the colour of your pee to assess your state of hydration. Although mine was in the 'sufficiently hydrated' class, it's probably time for another shot of the brunette nectar, I decide as I head back to the café.

'Still open?' asks a tall lady with ear-length blonde highlighted hair cut in that edgy style that's very short at the back and gets longer going round to the chin.

'Of course, yes, sorry,' I say, as it becomes clear Edith is not at the till. 'Have you been waiting long?'

The lady shakes her head.

'What would you like?' I ask.

She pushes forward a litre bottle of still water, which reminds me that I ought to have some of that, too, with my coffee in order to maintain my compliance with the pee poster. She asks for a small Americano. As I prepare her coffee I look around the café seating area for Edith and see her in the far corner, clearing tables of used cups and sandwich wrappings then furiously wiping the surfaces.

Edith is 'doing an Edith'. This eponymous activity has become recognised amongst the volunteers due to her matronly standards of cleanliness and, whenever there are no customers in the café, picking up a cloth and attacking the tables, getting so absorbed in her task that she forgets to keep an eye on the tills.

'That's £3.20, please,' I say as I hand my customer her Americano. 'Enjoy your drinks.'

Edith returns and she subjects her cloth to a torture on the level of water boarding by repeatedly soaking it under the tap and squeezing it mercilessly, as I continue to serve.

Towards the end of my shift I see a man with stud and ring-encircled ears, pushing round a buggy where a toddler stares out from the cosiness of his blue fleece carapace. The man brings his purchases to the counter. The toddler continues to stare at me and I wonder if I've grown horns.

'If you change that sandwich for one in the big chiller and swap the ordinary crisps for the low fat ones, you'd get the meal deal,' I advise.

'What's wrong with these?' he asks pointing to his selection of choice.

'Nothing. But they'll cost you more because they're not in the meal deal due to their higher fat content,' I advise further.

As the man stares at me, the provenance of his child's behaviour becomes clear.

'I think I can make these decisions for myself.'

Good point, I suppose, although a dissent from the conventions of twenty-first century healthy living. I smile and nod.

'And a latte, too, please. Large one. Three sugars,' he says, underscoring his point.

I nod again and take a large cup, place it under the nozzle, tap the large latte icon and as the frothy mixture of milk and coffee swirl downwards to their cardboard goal, four eyes are removed from me to the machine.

'And a banana, please, for the wee one,' the man says, nodding to the toddler, as I put the hot drink on the counter.

Ah, his concession to healthy living. All is not lost. I add it all up on the till, take his money and give him the change.

'Can I help you take these over to a table?' I ask.

I settle them down with their meals and the latte, and we exchange smiles – the toddler, too – ending my shift on a note both rewarding and edifying for me, and I resolve to be mindful of people's tastes while encouraging uptake of healthier foods.

Although one of the organisations I worked for before I retired offered its staff one day's paid leave each year to work for a charity, I wasn't aware then of the far-reaching benefits brought by volunteering, and I doubt I was alone in that ignorance. Raising awareness of the impact of volunteering, and the benefits obtained by communities and the volunteers themselves, may enable governments to capture the enormous potential in voluntary work.

As well as providing an excuse to buy more pairs of Pepes and boots, I've found that voluntary work meets a number of psychological needs. For example, I feel more connected now to both my community and to individual people with whom I have made friends, and this makes me feel that I matter to them, needs I'd identified during my long woodland walks.

Giving my time and expertise helps the charity café provide a service to hospital staff, patients and visitors, enabling hospital funds to grow, and so shows me that what I do contributes to the greater purpose of helping others, while I've also learned how to nurture a bean-to-cup coffee machine and to navigate a passable line between organisational policies and customer preferences.

And there's more: I am an introvert and as enlivening at parties as a Wagner opera, so it surprises me which of my duties I find most fulfilling. Maybe it's because each customer contact rarely lasts longer than the time it takes to make a large latte with an extra shot and hazelnut syrup; or maybe it reflects an increase in my self-esteem, but what gives me the greatest reward is meeting and assisting people every minute of my volunteering day.

15

THE WRONG NEST:
HOW TO REINVENT YOURSELF

'To exist is to change, to change is to mature, to mature is to go on creating oneself endlessly.'

HENRI BERGSON

My youngest child, Alex, at the time a student in Aberdeen, had contacted me through the twenty-first century's mecca of social media, Facebook. Like these wee sachets of coffee you find in a Travelodge it's tasteless but free, instant and alluringly functional.

'Hey, mummy, would you be my guarantor for my new flat and what shall I say your occupation is?'

'Hi, Ali, yes, okay. Does that mean I have to pay up if you trash it?'

'Yes, mummy. Shall I say you're a vet?'

'Um, well, I'm not a vet, well not a practising vet, any more. Is it a warm flat?'

'Yes, mummy. So shall I say you're a retired vet?'

'Hmm. Makes me feel old. Are you finding time to cook good meals?'

'Yes, mummy. Shall I say you're a volunteer then. Or a pony breeder. Or you write sometimes?'

You know, of course, that all through life, all the way from your slippery neonatal beginnings to the moment you're taken in a box to the funeral parlour, you metamorphose into different versions of yourself; a predetermined fundamental that to stand in the way of would be as successful as holding up a Japanese bullet train with your bare hands or averting Donald Trump from building walls. Baby, child, adolescent, adult and older, decrepit adult are the inevitable forms we will take if we reach the four score years that, God willing, we might have.

But this isn't self-reinvention. Nor is changing your job or appearance, your hair or teeth or whom you hang out with. These may help you get closer to your identity, but whatever this is takes some drilling down. And while our work or role gives us a social identity and defines what we are in our communities, it does not describe our inner being – the who we are – and nor does it reveal our destiny – the things we are able to accomplish. I suppose I'm still struggling to work it out; like I always struggled to play the piano with both hands while looking at music, and to be any good at reaching then nurturing an awareness of self is something, like piano playing or horse riding, you must start when you're very young.

'To be what we are, and to become what we are capable of becoming, is the only end in life.'

ROBERT LOUIS STEVENSON

In *The Ugly Duckling,* Hans Christian Andersen's tale of the abused and rejected duckling who grows into a beautiful swan, there is a message about how we see ourselves, and what happens when we believe and internalise what other people say about us. It shows that the ways in which other people respond to us, whether that is positively and with acceptance or with unkindness and cruelty, influence our appearance, behaviour and self-esteem.

The Ugly Duckling has been criticised for its apparent message that it was as a result of the protagonist's DNA that he gained dignity. But although the ugly bird turned into a lovely bird, accepted by his peers, the protagonist's real transformation lay in his self-discovery, which Hans Christian Andersen implied had been the route to his own success. It wasn't just the species the ugly duckling belonged to that allowed him to flourish: he also developed and maintained his self-belief in the face of abuse and hardship.

'Success is going from failure to failure with no loss of enthusiasm.'

ATTRIBUTED TO ABRAHAM LINCOLN

Religion dominated my earliest self-awareness, like too much of these artificially flavoured syrups you squirt into your cappuccino, so that worship and reading the Bible and singing hymns brought an element to self-reflection that wasn't the real thing. It seemed to me that church-going contained insincere elements and while religious practices may bring out the best in us as a species, encourage cooperation in a community, tend and befriend rather than fight or flight, I became aware of the hypocrisy that can creep into these arrangements like mould growing on four-day-old breakfast rolls.

The religious imperative robbed me of one of only two school-free days in the week and convinced me that just one molecule of alcohol would transform me into a reckless reprobate; and that going outside to play on Sundays leads to moral disintegration; and that in Church a girl's head must be covered with something itchy and pink and fantastically stupid. It wasn't until I was about thirteen that Sunday worship and Sunday school and choir practice became negotiable with my parents and therefore disappeared from my list of things I had to do, like twice-daily teeth cleaning and writing thank-you letters after birthdays and Christmas.

But my early church-going left me with a spirituality that runs through my identity like 'a present from Skegness' in a stick of rock. It endowed me with an aim to be compassionate towards others, to nurture empathy, social responsibility and a set of behaviours and ways of being that, although they reflect the teachings of Christ, they are basic good citizenship; humanist. So if you remove all the difficult-to-believe stuff about the religion into which I was born, it boils down to being a nice, kind person, and although I don't know about other religions in detail, I would think that they have similar ideologies at their roots.

'Remember who you are' was the phrase my parents said after I'd enjoyed some horseplay with neighbouring children and come home scruffy and undignified and with the glow of having had fun with friends. 'Remember who you are' implied that I knew who the who was that I must remember but the message, as clear as the Ribena used for communion, was that my friends were not really my peers. I should behave with more restraint. In the village but not of the village.

This sense of being something-not-like-others transmogrified to a raw realisation of my relatively meagre roots when I was later sent to a private school to rub my home-knitted navy cardigan-clad shoulders with the offspring of the more privileged, the urban and urbane, children furnished with bespoke shoes and satchels and expense accounts at the school outfitter and even turquoise ink for their fountain pens. Children whose names had been put down for the school at birth and not when their parents accepted that a state education of 1960s rural Scotland may impose limitations on its alumni and keep doors, which the fee-paying sector took off the hinges for their cherished privileged, firmly locked. How different a timbre then had, 'Remember who you are'.

This awareness of being born in an environment where I didn't belong underscored my loneliness at school and the irony that I didn't want to be with classmates who were different from me, but back with the friends I mustn't be the same as. I felt unassimilable into either group and hovered between them in a no man's land of not belonging.

My mother remarked on my 'wanting' to be different, as if being the odd kid in school and the weird one at home was something, like boiled egg for breakfast or straight-leg jeans, I selected and not things I had had at birth along with AB rhesus positive blood and blue eyes. Indeed, I felt different to my sister, brother and parents: a child and grandchild of city dwellers who were puzzled at my androgyny and longing to be with animals and in the countryside amongst vistas of green and brown and purple, and who probably hoped I'd grow out of all that. Trees and long, narrow, winding lanes with high verges and hedges of hawthorn and beech, and old roads where grass and moss poke between the cracks in the tarmac; banks flowing with rhododendrons, crumbling lichen-laden walls, random rabbit holes and twisting streams; all these things lifted my spirits as effectively as the sudden alleviation of some grave concern.

At about eleven years old I found a friend, Virginia, whose boyish mores and makeup mirrored mine, and an amorphous awareness of what might be termed my identity sprouted from my melancholy. About the same time, we moved to a house in the middle of nowhere and just five minutes drive from the prestigious school and where there were trees to climb and burns where my reed boats might eventually reach the Tay and where I could be like the boy I felt I should have been. As I felt the ease you get when you lie in spring sunshine after a hard, grey winter and feel every tendon, ligament and coiled up muscle disentangle, I began to feel justified in my tacit outrage against oppressive attitudes towards girls, young humans who were not allowed to behave with the freedom bestowed on boys.

The other family imperative throughout my childhood was the doctrine of unremitting hard work, the understanding that excellence is a habit, which squeezed between the base pairs of my DNA. As a result, at school I got a reputation for being brainy, although it was more because of the aforementioned hard work rather than any innate superior intellect. Listen in class. Learn. Revise. Do well in exams. It soon became clear to me that pupils who scored higher in exams went on to study sciences and it was the prejudice held up as a universal truth that arts subjects were interesting but if you were more academically able you studied sciences, that played a role in my ultimate career as a veterinary surgeon. So it's probably time I spilt the beans: although I loved animals and natural history, I became a vet because, in some small measure, I could.

All the while, within me, a quiet observer of the truth dropped hints that although biology, physics and chemistry were fascinating subjects, it was my school English lessons that illuminated elements of being human for me, enriched my soul and ignited my imagination. Of all my mentors, it was my English teacher, Mrs C, I remember most, an inspiring if redoubtable lady with her long skirts and flat lace-up shoes and hair scraped back in a low bun as dour as the Perthshire sky. She, and the novels and plays and poetry we studied together, gave me insights into the inscrutable, explained how to negotiate a path through life, helped me work out who I was and to understand and feel proud of my eccentricities and flaws. Through these texts I met people, places and ways of life that otherwise I may never have known; learned about other people's experiences, things I could relate to. Truths about the human condition were revealed to me and how best to respond to inevitabilities like a wet summer, ageing and the anticlimax of Christmas.

Both science and art provide us with an understanding of ourselves and our environment: science helps explain phenomena around us, while the literary masters, in the ways they use words to inspire thought and disclose the width and depth of emotion, describe the world and what it means to be human. We need both. But the disunion between art and science, borne out of increasing specialisation, no longer allows development of people like Leonardo da Vinci who was at once a painter, inventor and mathematician.

Of course, when you achieve something you have worked long and hard for, your identity changes its tone, and I was conscious that being accepted into a profession and practising as a vet altered the way I behaved. People responded to me in a different way and, indeed, my sense of who I was changed with membership of this profession, but I couldn't ignore a feeling of misalignment, of ignoring my destiny, of a need for re-calibration. It was like living with a sensitivity to some element in your diet that you thrive on but fails to make you feel quite right.

Discussing with fellow vets books I'd read or plays I'd been to or poetry I enjoyed seemed bohemian, pretentious, and was often met with an axiomatically disengaged 'oh that's nice'. Similarly, the artistically-minded responded to my non-veterinary interests with the suspicion you might have for someone who flirts with you at a party but who you know has no intentions of anything more serious. Throughout my veterinary career, the disconnect between what truly ignited me and the role I had chosen became more and more difficult to ignore. It felt right to immerse myself in literature and it was an odd contradiction that when I later studied an arts degree by distance learning, I suffered a crisis of self-doubt about who I really was and how, in the past, I had betrayed myself in pursuit of social recognition of academic achievement.

> 'Failure is simply the opportunity to begin again, this time more intelligently.'
>
> **HENRY FORD**

Maybe *The Ugly Duckling* inspired Winston Churchill who, in the early years of the twentieth century, was the Conservative Party's big cheese and at only thirty-six, was appointed First Lord of the Admiralty. Then, four years later, he was held responsible for the calamitous Gallipoli landings which led to his demotion.

But Churchill used this failure as the driver to show others the strengths that he knew he had. Throughout the First World War, instead of lounging around with some of his fellow aristocrats, he chose to serve in front-line positions, seeing some brutal action in France. In doing so, he developed his skills of determination and leadership, gaining the recognition and respect of his peers and pushing himself to perform at higher levels to become the person he knew he could be. He went on to address Parliament on a regular basis, reviving his political career, restoring his reputation with the British public and, of course, becoming Prime Minister.

Churchill stuck to his convictions. When one path closed, he found another through hard work and determination. And, of course, the arch personal re-inventor must be Dickens's Ebenezer Scrooge, the mean, cruel, socially-isolated yet highly successful businessman whose epiphany, thanks to a triumvirate of Christmas ghosts, led to his transformation to a warm and kind benefactor.

Many of us have endured 'wilderness years' as Churchill referred to his life between the World Wars. Maybe you're in a job that just isn't you, or your skill set no longer matches your employer's needs. Maybe your goals, your passions have slipped behind frosted glass, you've lost your way and you're starting to wonder if you'd hatched from an egg that rolled into the wrong nest.

With a degree of job dissatisfaction in the veterinary and many other professions, it is no longer inevitable that you must occupy until you retire the role you trained for as a teenager. Indeed, it does seem inappropriate that schools require you to make decisions at a young age about a career that is expected to last decades. By the time we have matured and metamorphosed into more enlightened and self-aware versions of ourselves, we find we have a way of life that is not our destiny.

Developing and leading out what is within you and removing yourself from emotional or mental stagnation, are not the province of the weak and flaky but of those who are perceptive, cognisant and have the courage to move out of a well-trodden route and path of least resistance. You don't need to be young to do it. Students like myself, so mature that we flow out of the fridge with three-week-old camembert, have grown in number with the opportunities for re-training. And as we, generally but not in every case, live longer, more of us after retirement are exploring opportunities and finding environments and activities that act on our souls like yeast on dough.

'It is never too late to be what you might have been.'

GEORGE ELIOT

I suppose I knew all along that at the core of my being was creativity. I know I am not alone in finding that creating something, or restoring something old and unloved and turning it into a useful or decorative thing, gives an achievable challenge, and focussing on that to the exclusion of anything else brings the well-being of a bracing walk followed by curling up in front of a log fire. But I wasn't able to do much about exploring that part of my identity while I needed to keep earning what I earned; career change almost always involves a sharp drop in income. And it wasn't just money that held me back. In spite of my doubts and limitations to self-belief, and the tried and tested, nicely-furnished rut that I found difficult to crawl out of, there was so much I enjoyed about being a vet. A danger that I might be heading towards self-immolation occurred to me besides the forfeiture in letting go of all my earlier achievements. Kipling's advice to 'start again at your beginnings and never breathe a word about your loss' seemed difficult to take. And, more than that, I needed a legitimate vision of myself, who I was, before I could abandon the social identity I had worked so hard for.

Of course, I dreamed a bit throughout my career and, for many years, well into my fifties, I still had the ambitions I'd had as a teenager, while acknowledging that my chances of realising them had become next to non-existent. Although I would occasionally idle through the job vacancies in the veterinary press and other publications and catch myself considering the most unlikely roles, this imaginative self-belief soon tiptoed out of consciousness and realism bulldozed in, reminding me that I was unlikely to become a show jumper or bacteriologist or a veterinary dentist capable of root canal treatment in the Sumatran tiger.

But it was at a retirement seminar that I gained the sense of fresh purpose of a spaniel seeing a pheasant fall out the sky. By then my self-awareness had matured and I felt able to let go of the past, and with that came the relief in swapping social status for expectations of me that didn't exceed a hot cappuccino with a generous sprinkling of chocolate.

I am proud to say I volunteer in a local charity café and that I love to read and study literature, do some writing and breed ponies. Sharing and comparing life experiences with a broad range of people has given me deeper connections with them, and others, it seems to me, reciprocate this. Altogether the world feels less lonely. I have a greater awareness of self-worth, too, although I'm still quirky and feel drawn to the same attributes in others.

Wisdom, like wrinkles and receding gums, comes with age and besides a richer self-knowledge we come to recognise useful truths, like everything changes with time, whatever you think matters doesn't, criticism can sometimes be rooted in envy, and the only useful presents as we get older are those for eating or drinking or showering. And although my self-reinvention continues its fine-tuning, my identity and I have declared peace; living in harmony, growing old together.

BIBLIOGRAPHY

CHAPTER TWO

Against all odds: The story of Aleen Cust (2018) The
   Veterinary Record   https://www.vetrecordjobs.com/
   myvetfuture/article/story-of-aleen-cust-britains-first-
   woman-vet/

CHAPTER FOUR

Tam O' Shanter. The Scottish Poetry Library
https://www.scottishpoetrylibrary.org.uk/poem/tam-o-
   shanter-tale/

CHAPTER SIX

What is wellness. Global Wellness Institute https://
   globalwellnessinstitute.org/what-is-wellness/
Psychology Today (2020) Positive Psychology https://www.
   psychologytoday.com/gb/basics/positive-psychology
Mind Matters: New Mental Health Initiative Launched

(2014) Royal College of Veterinary Surgeons https://www.rcvs.org.uk/news-and-views/news/mind-matters-initiative-new-veterinary-mental-health-and/

Roberts, A (1981) The 1763 Committee on Madhouses and the 1774 Madhouses Act. Middlesex University http://studymore.org.uk/2_2.htm

Smith, Matthew (2014) The Long, Mad Century. Psychology Today https://www.psychologytoday.com/gb/blog/short-history-mental-health/201408/the-long-mad-century

Sunrise House (2020) The History and Evolution of Mental Health and Treatment https://sunrisehouse.com/research/history-evolution-mental-health-treatment/

Vetlife. https://www.vetlife.org.uk/

Wikipedia. Flow. https://en.wikipedia.org/wiki/Flow_(psychology)

CHAPTER EIGHT

Dignitas http://www.dignitas.ch/?lang=en

Dignity in Dying https://www.dignityindying.org.uk/

Good Medical Practice. General Medical Council.https://www.gmc-uk.org/ethical-guidance/ethical-guidance-for-doctors/good-medical-practice

Harris, D., Richard, B., Khanna, P. (2006) Assisted dying: the ongoing debate (2006) Postgraduate Medical Journal https://www.ncbi.nlm.nih.gov/pmc/articles/PMC2585714/

Not Dead Yet UK http://notdeadyetuk.org/

Code of Professional Conduct for Veterinary Surgeons. Royal College of Veterinary Surgeons https://www.rcvs.

org.uk/setting-standards/advice-and-guidance/code-of-professional-conduct-for-veterinary-surgeons/

CHAPTER NINE

Wikipedia https://www.wikipedia.org/

CHAPTER TEN

Hugo, Kristin (2016) Tiny but mighty: this ancient Greek horse still exists today. National Geographic https://www.nationalgeographic.com/news/2016/09/skyros-ponies-horses-rare-breed/

The Rare Breeds Survival Trust https://www.rbst.org.uk/

CHAPTER ELEVEN

Macer, Richard, (2019) How a gender war sent the Morris Dancing World Hopping Mad. The Guardian https://www.theguardian.com/stage/2019/mar/29/morris-dancing-gender-women

The Morris Federation https://www.morrisfed.org.uk/

The Morris Ring https://themorrisring.org/

CHAPTER TWELVE

Falkingham, Liz (2017) Natural Horsemanship: What does it really mean? Horse and Hound https://www.horseandhound.co.uk/features/what-is-natural-horsemanship-533340

Jessop, Don (2017) Beginner's guide to Natural Horsemanship. Don JessopBreakthroughGuy https://medium.com/@DonJessop/beginners-guide-to-natural-horsemanship-by-don-jessop-1a462b7bf9e9

Parelli, P. (2008) Parelli's Secret. An introduction to

Natural Horsemanship. DVD produced by Horse and Country, horse and country.tv

Monty Roberts https://montyroberts.com/about-monty-roberts/

The Open College of Equine Studies (2005) The Theory of Learning and Application to the Training of Horses, Module 24, Bsc(Hons) Equine Science, Boxted, Bury St Edmunds, Suffolk.

Turner, M., Whitehead, I., Millard, N. (2006) The Effects of public funding on farmers' attitudes to farm diversification. University of Exeter. https://core.ac.uk/download/pdf/6429749.pdf

CHAPTER THIRTEEN

BBC (2014) WW2 People's War https://www.bbc.co.uk/history/ww2peopleswar/timeline/factfiles/nonflash/a1120861.shtml

Longden, Sean (2007) Hitler's British Slaves. Constable, London

CHAPTER FOURTEEN

National Council for Voluntary Organisations https://www.ncvo.org.uk/

The Royal Voluntary Service https://www.royalvoluntaryservice.org.uk/

The Volunteer Hospitals Database http://www.hospitalsdatabase.lshtm.ac.uk/the-voluntary-hospitals-in-history.php

CHAPTER FIFTEEN

Brainpickings https://www.brainpickings.org/2016/03/02/
  amelie-rorty-the-identities-of-persons/

Hasa (2016) What is the moral of the ugly duckling.
  Pediaa   https://pediaa.com/what-is-the-moral-of-the-
  ugly-duckling/

OpenLearn. The Open University. Identity in Question
  https://www.open.edu/openlearn/people-politics-law/
  politics-policy-people/sociology/identity-question/
  content-section-1.1

Popova, Maria (2016) What makes a person: The seven
  layers of identity in literature and life.

Wikipedia Winston Churchill. https://en.wikipedia.org/
  wiki/Winston_Churchill

About 40 years ago, I began compiling a Commonplace
Book. The quotations in it that I have used here can also
be found at brainyquote.com, quoteinvestigator.com,
libquotes.com and wikiquote.com.